In the Light of Thought

"A rush of thoughts is the only conceivable prosperity that can come to us."

Ralph Waldo Emerson

In the Light of Thought:
APHORISMS AND REFLECTIONS

by
John Sampson

With a foreword by
JOHN WALTERS
author of "Light in the Window" and "The Essence of Buddhism"

INDIANTOWN

Indiantown Printing, Inc.
Indiantown, Florida
33456

To my sister Hilda,
an unfailing source of comfort and help.

FOREWORD

One of the more talented journalists of the English-speaking world, John Sampson has turned out, in some ways, an uncomfortable, challenging book. It is not still another volume of happy, comfortable thoughts, of consoling reflections, to be placed alongside the works of those who believe this to be best of all possible worlds.

John Sampson utilizes the deceptive simplicity of the aphorism to deflate our sense of self-importance and to question the validity of many of the generally accepted values of our civilization. Many of his reflections tear into smug and cherished conceptions of philosophy, religion, history, politics, and human conduct. Such fusillades will fill you with self-questioning and should awaken the slumbering intellect to exciting reflections on scores of problems and topics. Then the lucid expressions of his own rational mysticism are likely to inspire you.

To digest masses of Sampsonian capsules in one gulp, as it were, would not be easy; for nearly every one of these stimulates a new stream of thought. Thus the author has sensibly, and even mercifully, interspersed his aphorisms with delightful literary vignettes. There is an interval for a little essay on Horace Walpole or Jane Austen, or for some unusual reminiscence of Sampson himself. Then the aphorisms start again. As you read on, the author seems to become more and more of a friend. You eventually come to appreciate him as no mean cynic, but an idealist refined by a passionate devotion to truth.

What is John Sampson like? To the journalists of New York, Washington and London, he is a tall, rather sardonic figure who asks politicians, diplomats and others awkward questions as he seeks news for his widely read British newspaper. While popular with his colleagues and socially charming in their company, he has a tendency suddenly to disappear at the height of convivial gatherings for the company of a book. As a devoted student of history and art, he spends much of his spare time in travel, usually alone. For years he haunted Italy, particularly Venice. But when Sampson is on his cultural prowls he could turn up anywhere. Once to my amazement I bumped into him outside a mosque in Tangier, Morocco.

John Sampson is a native of Liverpool, the ugly and misty English seaport which has produced scores of clever, unusual people, including the Beatles. He lives in New York with a sister, several cats and a fascinating personal library. First Sampson worked for the American press, then later became a special correspondent for important British newspapers, quickly winning respect as an authority on the United States.

Although some of Sampson's aphorisms seem hard, they cannot conceal his affection, understanding and sympathy with human nature in all its trials and weaknesses. Indeed, he is furtively an exceptionally kind and generous person. He detests the proud, the pompous and the spurious "successes" of the world. He is quick to identify the hypocrites, the poseurs.

"In the Light of Thought" is no conducted tour of Disneyland but a confrontation with hard realities.

John Walters

London, England

INTRODUCTION

I once asked Dame Edith Sitwell what her advice would be to a young writer, then settled back to hear her discourse learnedly on style. Her answer was, "Never throw anything away." That was all.

So here they are, my reflections on life and people, which partly owe their existence to Dame Edith. Most of them were jotted down at odd moments and odd places, both in America and abroad, with no thought then of publication or of entertaining and influencing others. All were addressed to myself either as criteria of conduct or commentaries on life. Only a few reflect the events I was writing about as a British correspondent. This should not be surprising. These were events well and ably reported, often by writers better equipped to convey the excitement and significance of them than myself. I was looking for something else.

The misfortune of our time is that people have been too carried away by events—have become so absorbed, in fact, in matters of concern to the country that they have ceased to meditate over what is vital to themselves. The world has been too much with us, and we have been apt to miss the inward insights that may, after all, be more important to our happiness and well-being. "The greatest thing in the world," says Montaigne, "is to know how to belong to ourselves."

I hope readers will not be repelled by the aphoristic form in which I have cast many of my musings, serious and lighthearted. La Rochefoucauld, Vauvenargues, La Bruyere, Joubert, Chamfort, all have given the form a measure of taste and respectability. In fact, wrote Lord Morley in "Oracles on Man and Government," it became in such hands a peculiar French art, arising out of their inability to escape from the restraints of their time and express themselves in poetry. In our own time, so inimical to poetry, sentiment and sermonizing, the lowly aphorism again emerges as a convenient vehicle of thought. The danger, I fear, is that the writer may strain for "wit and wisdom" at the expense of sincerity. I hope I may be spared that imputation.

John Sampson

New Dorp, Staten Island, N. Y.

In the Light of Thought

Never worry about apparent caprices in those we love. Such is the penalty of familiar friendship. It is a kind of compliment in friends not always to show us their pleasantest manners.

One of the greatest afflictions of our time is dwelling on things we *want* and not on things we *have*. When we are asked to thank God for our blessings, is this not another way of remembering them?

I walk amid the graves and see nothing but the trees, the flowers, the brook, the squirrels, the chipmunks, the birds,—everything that proclaims the newness of life.

One is sustained by the imagination in youth, by the memory in age.

Not discovering one's ideal woman in life may not be

conducive to perfect happiness. But it produces the next best thing—a perpetual state of hope.

This waiting for age to supply experience to youth is one of the greatest tragedies of our time.

Just as one may feel murderous and not be guilty of murder, so one can feel jealous and not be guilty of jealousy.

A woman would much sooner think she has given up wicked ways than that she has never acquired any.

You can be fairly sure that, if you say something innocent to a person that causes him to be violently angry, you have hit upon the truth.

This poor man who bends so lovingly over this grave —is there not someone away from here to whom he can devote his remaining years to make happy? She to whom he pays homage is beyond the consciousness of his grief. No neglect that he might have committed while she was living can be undone now. No cruelty can be repaired, no omission supplied, no thoughtless word taken back. But if his beloved had a voice it would be to implore him to make haste and administer kindness to one in need of it. He, the mourner, will be here soon enough.

Beware of a brilliant man. Being overconfident, he depends too much on himself, ignores reality and takes heedless risks. Brilliance is often but an attribute of one who is wrong spectacularly.

We pray to God that, by some miracle, something will happen that we have thought impossible. And, behold, the miracle occurs—we find within ourselves the power to do it!

Never worry about the consequences of an act as long as it is morally right. The consequences are bound to be right too, even though different from what we expect.

Learn the lesson of gradualness. See how the seasons evolve and day merges into night and night into day and how youth grows imperceptibly into manhood. So it should be in all the changes we undertake.

I listened to a young woman tell me there was no God. She was pitting her 21 years of error and ignorance against 4000 years of wisdom and experience.

The worst habit in the world for a man in love is keeping a picture of his beloved continually before him. He then dwells on virtues that the subject may not possess, and sees her in an attitude of meekness and silence that may be ludicrously false.

For half a century England has been plagued by governments that plunged her into impossible situations, either through stupidity or incompetence, then called upon the people to make heroic exertions to get the country out of the mess.

When we thank God for having rejected our prayer, then we are living in perfect accord with divine wisdom.

She was a sturdy, not unattractive girl in her late twenties, leading a troop of fifteen schoolgirls on a hike through the Black Forest. Her short-cropped hair, her seriousness, her dedication, her undoubted flair for leadership, her air of masculinity concealing what I was sure were deep wells of tenderness,—all conjured up in my mind a Teutonic Joan of Arc. Her orders were sharp and instantly obeyed. The little girls paused at a lake to look at a dead fish, which, poor creature, received far more attention when dead than it ever had while living, in this respect not unlike many people. Their leader waited patiently for them on the upper bank, not partaking in their frolic, though not intolerant of it. When one of her charges got into danger while wading, she kicked off her shoes and went to her help. There was nothing, you felt, she was incapable of doing to fulfill her responsibility. How many other rustic Joans have degenerated to this? Or is 'degenerated' unfair? Only a great occasion, perhaps, is wanting to call them to a historic stage. Or the occasion comes and an overwhelming host of frustrations, such as only an unbelieving, jeering, conceited, sophisticated age can produce, arise to defeat them.

Man's success in rocketing into space must, perforce, imply a corresponding ability to destroy himself. Are the gods mocking us? Is this their eternal surety that heaven will remain inviolate?

Those people who never worry always leave it to others.

Democratic governments too often degenerate into multiple tyrannies.

The secret of getting along with people is not seeing too much of them.

Take everything life offers, knowing always there is ample good in it.

The only wisdom is in doubting.

I am more interested in those watching beautiful works of art than in the works themselves. What painting of a woman, no matter by what hand, can compare to a beautiful woman looking at it, alive, graceful, mysterious?

What is important to a person is not whether he believes in Christ, Mahomet, Buddha or some other religious leader, but whether he possesses the God-consciousness to make him a patient, kind, compassionate being.

I walk a lot in the cemetery to keep out of it longer.

Try to live every day as if seeing everything for the first time.

Perfection is impossible in people. We lose so much by looking for so much.

In the Cathedral of Milan there was something more awe-inspiring in a statue with a white sheet over it than all the others that were uncovered. So mystery bestows an enormous measure of interest, whether it is a masterpiece by an unknown hand, an unsolved murder, a strange woman.

When one is uncertain what to do, it is best to postpone a decision until the last, when circumstances may be such that all uncertainty vanishes.

Another visit to Concord. How much I revere Emerson and Thoreau! Thoreau's personal declaration of independence, beautifully set down in the first chapter of "Walden," should be a more memorable event to Concord than the skirmish at the old North Bridge that led to the country's declaration of independence. Yet today the bridge is a national shrine while the pond is a bathing beach pungent with the smell of hot-dogs.

Thoreau's fellow-townsmen looked upon him as an ill-clothed, eccentric fellow who had thrown away a Harvard education and other advantages to ramble in the woods; and every year since his death only a remnant of his countrymen ever bother to turn to his books or heed him if they do. But he has a message for everyone, not necessarily to seek solitude—though God knows that is needed nowadays—but to follow one's genius to the end, no matter how poor it may make us materially and in the opinion of our friends.

There is nothing particularly new in his philosophy. It is merely a seeking for the divinity in each of us. It has been preached by Christ and most of the wise men of the world for the past 2000 years. But today, with all our vaunted progress, the conflict between citizen and state is more intense than it ever was; and the man who can imbue his fellow-beings with the courage and faith to do what they want is a benefactor supreme. It is not always necessary to retire to the woods; independence can be attained in easier ways than that. If it is solitude we wish, most of us can have that merely by shutting the door and turning off the radio or television.

We shall win the stars but forfeit heaven.

I sometimes wonder if there is not more Christianity in Communism, outwardly atheistic, than in capitalism, ostentatiously pious.

To admire all that is lovely in creation—flowers, cats, dogs, a lake, a sunset, a starry sky, a mountain peak,— is this not the highest kind of homage to God?

When a country sets out to fight for liberty everywhere, you can be sure it won't leave much anywhere.

I began life reading fairy tales. Thanks to science, I end by living them.

Snow-capped mountains thunder forth their eternal message of silence.

Life is too rich in things to come to waste time on what is past. Scrap everything that drags you back— outdated friendships, outmoded ideas, stale romances, old garments,—and start life afresh as often as needful.

There has been too much stress placed on the crucifixion of Christ, too little on the feasting, drinking and good companionship that preceded it.

A place or a person is important to me by the degree of thought it inspires.

The American way of life is no longer inspired by the noble principles of the Revolution, drawn from everything that was great in Anglo-Saxon thought, but is controlled by the catch-phrases of advertising, based on the proposition that people will do whatever you please as long as you have the money to make them.

Culture should be like a gentle rain, never visible like a dirty puddle of water, but seeping through a receptive soil to bring to fruition an abundance of beautiful thoughts.

Say a barbarian, cut off completely from civilization, were to contemplate, for the first time, a huge airliner idle on the ground. Would he not be forgiven if he insisted on its inability to fly? His disbelief would be overcome only by *seeing* it in flight. Are we not barbaric in matters of faith, refusing to believe something unless we see it, disregarding the testimony of those more knowing than ourselves?

The writing that is worth anything—that which is sincere and best echoes the writer's thoughts—has been hastily composed. Embellishments are meaningless unless they rise spontaneously, for anything that has been sought by long thinking is not worth the finding.

I have been reading the best books all my life, but there are so many I have not read that any 12-year-old child can say to me: "What! you've never read *that!*"

The most useful part about getting to know people is getting to know ourselves.

I talk to the woods, and they never talk back except in whispers; and often they nod their heads in good-natured agreement.

Looking back longingly in our lives to a time that is past is a sign of abnormality; and instead of being made the subject of stories and plays, even when they are well done, it should be treated with disdain. Every phase of our life offers an abundance of things that we later remember with pleasure, unencumbered, perhaps, by all that then gave us uneasiness and annoyance. It is certain that, at this very moment, quietly, almost unknowingly, numerous things are contributing to our happiness, the loss of any of which would grieve us. Learn to recognize and cherish these things now.

We count so many people friends who have never been put to the test of friendship.

A man is always stupid to marry. But from how many other stupidities does marriage save him?

There are forces within us that drive us to act sometimes in face of custom and common sense. A man can resist these forces and be as he was before; but he must be content to remain a person who has not completely realized everything within him, be that what it may.

The important thing for us is not to shape our actions in accordance with what others think of us—they generally think the worst, anyway,—but to do nothing except in accordance with the highest conception we have of ourselves.

Women in the Victorian time were anxious to make themselves out purer than what they were, whereas women today are anxious to make themselves more wicked.

How can one praise virtue that has never been tested? It would be like praising an army that has never seen a battlefield, or a ship that has never gone to sea.

My conscience is not the conscience that doth make cowards of us all, but the conscience that makes a servant of me, forcing me to do those things in which I have not the slightest interest.

A just appreciation of Horace Walpole must always depend upon a wise selection of his letters. I formed a poor judgment of him upon the first book of selections I read. It was devoted to letters illustrating Walpole's life, which was very humdrum and little different from the lives of other English gentlemen of the 18th Century. There is hardly an event in Walpole's life that stands out. He wrote some books that made little impression on his contemporaries and are forgotten now. He took an inactive part in politics. He never did or said anything that arrested public attention.

How then is Walpole important to us today? It is as a reporter and commentator of his own time. He was a newspaperman without a newspaper. He had a keen eye for seeing things and a quick pen for setting them down. We might wish at times that Walpole would be more serious and take a deeper interest in certain events or people, instead of skipping over them lightly. In one of his letters, he ascribes this to indifference, which he calls "the sole key to almost every action of my life for some time past, and I believe for all to come."

But this very indifference of Walpole was an aid to his objectivity as a journalist. Nowhere does he become so absorbed in anything—politics, literature, art, fashion, science,—that he is oblivious of other matters. He is interested in everything. And the variety of his interests is the charm of his letters.

To try to arouse our indignation by a recital of atrocities committed in a war, is like getting indignant over a pickpocket in hell.

The trouble with politicians is that they are so busy talking they never have time to think.

Worry is a blasphemous denial of God.

Why should I deplore differences with others when I find myself so difficult?

Noble speeches can be addressed only to audiences that have in themselves an element of nobility; great letters can be written only to friends who inspire in us the best.

The person who thinks his happiness permanent is just as foolish as the one who thinks his misery so.

The man who has by good fortune acquired a repu-

tation for shrewdness is fated never to lose it, for no
matter what stupidities and blunders he commits his
admirers will never acknowledge it but say rather: "Ah,
this is more of his shrewdness!" And in this they credit
themselves with shrewdness, too!

I would reverse the popular saying, "Where there's
life there's hope," and say, "Where there's hope there's
life." What does it matter if hope is unfulfilled? The
important thing is to be able to hope, and if one hope
is disappointed to laugh and go on to another.

One cannot be morally indignant without being morally
right.

I walk in the cemetery to be cheerful, and to console
myself with the thought that, no matter what worries I
may have, no matter how deeply I may think I am over-
whelmed by the pressure of duties, at least I am better
off than those among whom I tread. *They* do not have
the problem of earning enough to eat, of meeting bills
and taxes, of writing letters, of doing all those things
we find distasteful,—and behold, how low they lie! This
is the perfect peace to which many of us strive, and to
which all of us ultimately must come. But while God is
gracious to us let us enjoy the pleasures of the present,
and endure the accompanying burdens with a good heart.

When we are told how Socrates, as a soldier, once
stood outside his tent, all one day and all one night,
entranced in thought, while warriors gathered round
watching in awe, we are pleased not so much at this
spectacle of the great philosopher, but at the thought
that here, in the midst of war, a scene that the vulgar

might think was ludicrous could attract such a multitude of admirers. Is it small wonder that philosophy thrived in such an age?

What is the closest of all ties between a man and woman? Why, consciousness of a guilty secret!

How can someone criticize me effectively? By showing I have acted contrary to myself.

What we think are faults in others are only infirmities, to be pitied even when they wrong us.

My friend said that, to withdraw from the world and try to find peace within ourselves was an escape from reality. How wrong he was! To re-discover ourselves in the midst of a noisy world is the highest form of reality —indeed, the last and only good that may be attainable by any of us.

I left the restaurant without tipping the waitress, and did not remember until hours later, when it was too late to return. But the fact that I wanted to—that I felt terribly grieved by my omission—was not altogether displeasing. Here was a restaurant I seldom visited, a waitress I never expected to see again, and yet I was sorry, rather than glad, at my forgetfulness. Did it not prove that there was a well of good feeling in me, independent of fear or self-interest?

Remember, when you hear people talk learnedly about the prospect of peace or war, that war doesn't respond to reason. If it did, there wouldn't be war.

The philosophy of life is to take things as they come—cheerfully if possible, but always calmly.

———

Probe a person's life a little way and it's a comedy; probe a little further and it's a tragedy.

———

I am partial to the idea of kings but detest the worship of them.

———

It is the duty of statesmen to distinguish between a people restrained by too much order and a people endangered by too much freedom.

———

One of the charms of foreign travel is not knowing what people are saying.

———

Discuss a difficulty and it ceases to be one.

———

Most of the evils of life are in excess—parsimony that runs to greed, strictness to tyranny, generosity to recklessness, caution to cowardice, enthusiasm to fanaticism.

———

Behold these mourners coming to the graves of their lost ones, when they themselves are entombed in their own narrow thoughts, their prejudices and fears, their customs and habits, and have almost as little life and freedom as those they grieve for.

———

We can stretch out our lives—not forward, because that may be contrary to Nature, but backward as far as we wish to go. How? By ceasing some of those petty things that fill up so much of our lives and projecting our imagination to past times. We can do this by reading histories, memoirs or letters; by going to a picture gallery or museum; by visiting old churches or places associated with famous people. Indeed, we may know remote times better than those people did that actually lived in them, mingling behind the scenes and penetrating to the heart of great events in a way impossible to us if we had lived then. The age I know least about is the age I am living in. But how, it may be protested, can it be said you know such men as Caesar, Washington or Napoleon if you never saw them? I never saw Hitler or Mussolini, and yet I was their contemporary. Cromwell, who lived more than three centuries ago, I know better than either of these. So a man can be the contemporary of all the great people who ever lived, and know them as intimately as if he lived with them. It is done through the magic of the mind, the domain in which we truly live.

While others visit a graveyard seeking the dead, I go there seeking life.

When a thing loses its simplicity, it loses its reality.

Do things more from feeling and less from purpose.

Inspiration is more important than experience.

War may never be abolished, but sensible nations can keep out of it.

We can do things only within the limits of our nature. But let us be sure we touch those limits.

The purpose of argument is not to overcome an opposing will but to rouse kindred feelings.

Ambition is the compass of the soul.

Life is like a moving picture—it appears spontaneous as we experience it first, but viewing it over we see that everything was prearranged and that it goes forward with relentless purpose to a predetermined end.

It is not for us to regulate consequences; it is for us to do what is right.

Never trust to chance what can be gained by energy.

Youth should start out full of idealism so a little may flow over and make the world a better place.

Ghost-hunting in the Hampshire village of Chawton. Jane Austen is one of the most elusive of ghosts. Here in the cottage she shared with her mother and sister, it is easy to see Jane, her dark curls spilling from under a little cap, bending over her mahogany writing-desk at "Mansfield Park" or "Persuasion," then slipping the sheets under a blotter whenever the squeaking of a door announces a visitor.

There is still a squeaking door between Jane and those who try to discover how this simple young woman, with little schooling, no opportunity to travel beyond England and with a limited range of experience, could compose novels that exhibit an insight into human nature only a little below that of Shakespeare. None of her biographers have explained her completely. Only the letters Jane wrote to her sister Cassandra bring us close to her.

But these were not letters to posterity. They were letters to her family and about her family. They are almost entirely concerned with what she called "important nothings"—romance, marriage, births, deaths, cooking, dressmaking, shopping, holidays. Hers was the poetry of the commonplace. What was going on immediately about her was the real drama of life, not the shrill debates of Parliament or the Napoleonic battles raging across the Channel. These were to be left to the historian of events. She was the historian of the heart.

It is impossible, after reading the letters, to hold to the popular image of Jane as a shy, reclusive girl, silent in company, seldom venturing out of doors. She was a chatterbox, delighting in gossip. If the letters had come down to us unidentified, they must, inevitably, have been marked for destruction as the possession of a family who treasured them merely as sentimental trivia.

One shudders to think what would have happened if some rich, kindly person had recognized Jane's talents as a young girl and decided to "take her in hand." Well travelled and well read, with the highest education possible to a young woman of her time, she might then have written letters replete with clever observations of men and the world. But Jane Austen, the great portrayer of the comedy of manners, would have been lost to us.

There is no greater proof of incompetency than the disposition to meddle in another's affairs.

There is good in perceiving faults in others. We see how disagreeable they can be in ourselves.

Suspicion should never be an incentive to action.

Do not attend to dangers that lie far ahead for fear of missing those at hand.

———

No one can feel real love for another without the consciousness of reciprocated affection.

———

Many of the evils of this world come from those who know how to express themselves but not how to think.

———

A person never does a wrong because he knows it is wrong. He is driven to it by ambition, vanity, greed, selfishness, jealousy or ignorance.

———

Wise administration is knowing when to extend a helping hand and when to keep hands off.

———

A mind cannot rise higher than its own level.

———

Think of nations not as vague abstractions, such as England, France and Italy, but as peoples—the English, French, Italians,—whose lives and comforts must be of paramount concern.

———

Much of the advice we prescribe for others is only justification of ourselves.

———

A memorized speech comes from the mind, an extemporaneous one from the heart.

———

Getting on in life is largely a matter of making few mistakes and taking advantage of the other fellow's.

To be convinced of the inevitability of anything is just another way of wanting it to happen.

Petty people are destroyed by their own pettiness.

We should be conservative and progressive at the same time—conservative toward everything in the past worthwhile holding, progressive toward everything new that is worthwhile acquiring.

I lent a dime to someone desperately in need of it to telephone. He did not repay me. When I saw him next and remembered about it, I was troubled. Was I so petty as to worry about a dime? But there was something else behind my recollection—disenchantment with the borrower. Surely, such a person must lack a sense of gratitude and decency, manifest in more important matters than my dime.

What a torturing irony it is when, scorning money and the mean qualities that go with money, one finds all his aspirations dependent upon it.

It is not from men who openly advocate war but from men who hypocritically talk peace that the real menace to peace is to be found.

When I am in the right, I am not afraid of consequences. I let God take care of them.

Success depends as much upon recognizing our limitations as our potentialities.

Big words are only useful in cowing little people.

Worry when you can do something; don't worry when you can't.

Only God creates; the rest of us merely observe and imitate.

Apportion responsibility among many and it becomes the responsibility of none.

Always speak what is uppermost in your mind. Don't elaborate or grope for words. Come out with it straight. Other thoughts with other words will follow in the train of the first.

If you take into notice all the obstacles in the way of an enterprise, nothing would ever be done. But what matters how many obstacles there are as long as each can be surmounted?

Impress men with your integrity and they will follow you anywhere.

Next to having our jokes taken seriously, the worst misfortune is having our sentiments taken as jokes.

Peace cannot be safe unless it is grounded in justice—not justice according to the law but according to humanity.

Once I asked Sir Francis Goodhusband, a zealous

Christian, why it was that Christendom fostered more wars than other religions. He was much perturbed by the question. But I meant nothing disrespectful. If the question troubled Sir Francis, it troubled me too. The answer, surely, is that those nations professing Christianity are not truly Christian. There is little they do that can be reconciled to the spirit or teachings of Christ. They boast of playing the Good Samaritan in going to war to help another country. But nowhere in that parable is there mention of the Samaritan committing violence. He never bothered about the robbers. He was too busy ministering to their victim.

One should not brood over mistakes, for fear of not embarking on any action in which mistakes may occur.

Philanthropy is to be judged not so much by what is given as by what is left.

The force of example is always better than force itself.

Think only of the future insofar as doing right in the present.

Not to think is not to grieve.

Great progress in nations is nearly always attended by violence. Governments must be forced as often as they are persuaded.

For centuries, England has been rich in individualities —persons who have dared to act against her; and England has been great in finally recognizing and honoring them.

In "Historical Sketches of Statesmen," Lord Brougham had a rare opportunity of observing and judging many of the greatest men of history, being born in 1778 and dying in 1868—a lifetime of ninety years that brought him into contact with Fox, the younger Pitt, Burke, Canning, Lord North, Castlereagh, Erskine, Sheridan, Grattan, Wilberforce, Peel, Wellington, Grey, Palmerston. But he has succeeded throughout his three volumes in giving us only one perfect characterization— himself, the portrait of an insufferable bore.

Every sentence of Brougham's is labored and artificial. He seems to feel that it would be an unwarranted act of condescension and a breach of dignity to pass from vague generalities to specific illustrations. He speaks in one place of "a learned and eminently narrow-minded man," and by later mention of a dictionary leaves us to guess it is Samuel Johnson. He disdains to translate his French and Latin passages, as though the reader unversed in these languages has no business to be reading his book anyway.

Brougham can be best contrasted with Macaulay, his political friend and fellow contributor to the *Edinburgh Review*. It would be an education in writing to set the works of the two together and see what to imitate in one and avoid in the other. Nowhere does Brougham approach Macaulay's ease, naturalness, copiousness and clarity. Nowhere does he have those brief, vivid touches of characterization that brighten the pages of Macaulay, with the exception of his sketch on Castlereagh, whose blundering habit of speech and courage in facing the ridicule of Parliament under the handicap are very graphically described.

There is little outward difference between a fool and a Christian.

Never follow routine so closely that you have no time for unexpected and more important things.

The world answers more to human nature than to human intelligence. And the study of human nature is helped by history.

It is useless to deny that great civilizing force has always been attended by great military power.

Emerson's writings, alternately obscure and illuminating, are like a thunderstorm—a far-off rumbling, a darkening over, peals of thunder, then brilliant flashes of light.

When we do things from the heart, we are following God's way.

I detest those people who always know what is the proper thing to do—who are always so intent upon being correct that they forget ever to be kind and generous. "Show me the young man," said Robert Louis Stevenson, "who knows how to make a fool of himself."

Age does not always command veneration. Look at the oldest profession in the world.

Vanity is the product of ignorance, for when a man

touches the fringe of the great world of knowledge he cannot help feeling very insufficient and humble.

Beware of giving undue importance to things you don't understand.

Meddling and muddling—the two things go together.

Give your problems to time, the most divine thing we have because the most eternal.

There is no better spot to attack anyone in persuasive discourse than his vanity. Find out what he takes pride in most, compliment him on it (always justly because it is something wherein he excels), and you have disposed him in your favor. Often it may take much effort and engaging in long conversation before you draw out a person sufficiently to know what it is that is the object of his self-pride. Always there is something, perhaps on the surface, perhaps buried beneath a reserved character,—but always it is there. Find it. It is the secret of commanding people.

If criticism of me is wrong, I laugh at it; if right, I heed it.

We are always ready to be tolerant toward those with whom we agree.

The hardest task of one seeking the truth is to distinguish between cause and effect.

The English are actuated too much by a spirit of chivalry, undirected by reason. They are the only nation who could have admired the Charge of the Light Brigade without wanting to tear the idiots responsible for it to pieces.

I have generally found that if you do what is right today, even though the immediate consequences may seem foreboding, tomorrow can be trusted to bring us good.

Joseph Conrad's writing is like his beloved sea—sometimes quiet and beautiful and clear, then dark and angry and tempestuous; now lazily rolling against a headland, now swirling and boiling around it.

It lacked five minutes of departure from Milan when a pair of perspiring soldiers slid open the door of my first class compartment, saw I was alone and said something to me in Italian. Then one stood guard in the corridor, apparently to prevent anyone else from coming in while the other rushed off along the platform. Presently he returned with a puffing general, fat and pompous, followed by a pretty young woman of about 26, whom I guessed was his wife, and a boy of about 5 whom I assumed was their son. Two more privates labored after them with their baggage. The general stood in the corridor while the suitcases were heaved into the racks alongside mine. Then he snapped an order to his escort, who stood to attention, saluted and left.
 The general was soon engrossed in his paper in the window seat opposite mine. Not a word was exchanged with the wife and boy. The two sat alongside him. Occasionally the boy whispered to his mother, who whis-

pered back. An hour after leaving Milan, the general
removed a beribboned tunic and hung it on a peg near
the door. Then he fell asleep. Mother and boy continued
to whisper together, nervous about wakening him.

The train came into Verona. The platform noise awoke
the general, who let the window down to see where we
were. Then he growled something at his wife and child,
elbowed his way through a throng in the corridor and
climbed down onto the crowded platform. I saw him
speaking to a conductor. I surmised he was asking how
long we would be there. When I got out, I could see him
striding off to one of the waiting rooms.

In fifteen minutes, shrill whistles sounded along the
platform. Passengers clambered back on the train. Platform vendors hurried to windows where passengers were
still shrieking for soft drinks or sandwiches. Then the
long train pulled out.

Back in the compartment, the general's wife was at the
window glancing back at the platform. Son Enrico still
sat primly in his seat. The train gathered speed and his
mother slid back the door to peep into the corridor. Passengers were walking back from rear cars and re-entering
their compartments. No general appeared.

She stood there several minutes. Then she closed the
door and resumed her seat. The two continued whisper-
ing. Occasionally the mother would hear a step outside
and look up quickly. Then all was silence except for the
roar of the train racing toward Venice.

Poor Enrico looked so frightened I thought he would
burst any moment into tears. His mother patted him
gently on the hand but looked equally distraught. Neither
glanced at me. Plainly the time had come to speak. I
asked the mother in English if she had any money, and
when she shook her head uncomprehendingly I pulled out
my wallet, withdrew several Italian notes and extended
them to her.

A sudden look of terror crossed her lovely face. She leapt to her feet and grabbed the general's tunic from the hook. Quickly she ran through his pockets until she found what she wanted. It was a thick wad of money. She waved it at me gleefully, said something to Enrico and the two broke into laughter. They continued laughing and chatting all the way into Venice.

Outside the station, they scrambled merrily into a motorboat and shot off along the Grand Canal, waving and shouting to me in a gondola bobbing in their wake.

I saw them two days later on the Riva degli Schiavoni. They were walking in the crowd still clutching the general's tunic. They saw me and came up laughing, pouring out a long story in Italian in which I caught only the name Julietta. Then they began laughing again and I laughed too. I never saw them again.

Some virtues, like stars, are to be seen only when everything is darkest.

Life is like a bank—you get out of it what you put in.

I never argue; I merely state facts.

Never prophesy from reason, when chance and emotion are largely responsible for what happens.

There is an art to kidding a person—you must never touch upon the truth.

Far from being artificial, as its scoffers charge, the Victorian age was very close to reality because it was very close to God.

If a thing is told truthfully and deeply and sympathetically, it will be told dramatically.

What a feeble thing is friendship!—to be shattered by the slightest touch of jealousy, selfishness or self-interest.

To see deeply is to see beautifully.

What harm a man of integrity can wreak with a few careless remarks! Having a reputation for probity, he can pass judgment on people that is accepted more readily from him than from others, even though his opinions are palpably wrong.

The best national anthem?—the shortest.

Two things bring out the real character of a person—drink and sport.

We generally exercise our right to worship God as we please by not worshipping Him at all.

The degree of man's wickedness is determined by what he can get away with.

The most exalted things in life we never argue about.

What an awful world this would be if God did everything in accordance with our wishes!

You cannot suspend the precepts of Christ by an act of Parliament or of Congress.

———

Have not many great men achieved their ends by being great nuisances? Witness Paul of Tarsus. "We have found this man a perfect pest," the high priest complained to the Roman governor at Caesarea, according to the James Moffatt translation. Of course, he was. That's how he got a free voyage to Rome!

———

The English have so prided themselves on being good losers that they have ceased to be good winners.

———

How can you expect great deeds from men when there are no great women?

———

The only thing in the world you cannot change is the past—but you can change your attitude to it.

———

The decline of humor is one of the worst disasters of our time. We have all become too serious. We lack that delightful detachment to the cares of the world that made Addison so entertaining in his own time, and Goldsmith, and Sydney Smith, and Dickens, and Lewis Carroll, and Will Rogers. Humor has lost its spontaneity. It has become something thought up by gag-writers.

———

Look for the best from yourself, the worst from others.

———

It is a great mistake to try too hard. What each of us should learn is the importance of being indifferent.

The great heroes of history are usually represented in fiction and drama as too noble to be human or too human to be noble.

Change is the eternal order of Nature. Without it we should never have been born. Why then deplore our passing?

Let us have the power to fight when our own vital interests are violated; let us have the power to forbear when they are not.

What is remote always appears enchanting. At a distance we see heaven and earth uniting. As we come nearer, alas, heaven is as far off as ever.

They say this is the century of the common man. Would it were the century of the superior man!

Always have something to look forward to.

We should never question a fellow man's inalienable right to go to the devil.

Does not the magic of many things vanish when we name them?

Consider what an infinitesimal difference separates many things. Only one letter separates immorality and immortality, slaughter and laughter, the beast in us and the best in us, fiend and friend.

Ghost-hunting in St. Mark's Square. Petrarch perched between the bronze horses of the Cathedral. Byron limping across the square at midnight. Wagner listening to a band concert from a table at Florian's. Ruskin and Effie Gray emerging from the courtyard of the hotel that is now a bank.

And Sabina. Hardly a ghost. But she haunts me every time I go back—a tiny, disdainful presence on the great Piazza amid that ghostly assemblage.

I first saw Sabina in a flimsy summer dress, glancing languidly at the shopwindows under the arches, then turning into the Mercerie. She always said I followed her. Maybe I did, for when I spoke to her at the Rialto, she said plaintively: "Why did you let me walk all the way to the Rialto?"

We went that evening to the Casino, where she skipped from one roulette table to another, gambling away what money she could coax from me. We came back about 2 a.m. by gondola, she snuggled in my arms, nibbling at my ear and glancing back nervously from time to time at the gondolier. "I no like him," she whispered, running her fingers across her throat.

She was an Argentinean, traveling with her mother and father through Italy. She had stayed behind in Venice to pick up documents at the Argentine Consulate while her parents continued to Rome. It was the first time, I think, she had broken away from Latin restraint. She was making the most of it.

For a week she dominated my life. She planned our excursions, doled out my tips, bargained with shopkeepers. She was jealous, vain, selfish and shamelessly ignorant about history and art. In public she was always the lady, quiet and dignified. Alone, she was a little girl, alternately playful and tearful. She demanded an accounting of everything I did out of her presence, and expected, in return, a generous measure of jealousy and possessiveness from myself.

One hot afternoon, when I persuaded her to go off for an hour or two and leave me to rest, she remained away longer than we had arranged. It was obvious she expected me to create a scene on her return. I tried not to disappoint her and said some words sharply to her. She threw her arms about me, swore she had been true, hurled herself on the bed and cried, then rose up and poured out a torrent of abuse at me in Spanish. All the time, she was casting sly glances at herself in the full-length mirror. Her performance was worthy of a great actress. And she knew it.

She made me promise to "respect" her, then delighted in putting my forbearance to agonizing tests. She would suddenly let slip a couple of shoulder-straps and peel everything off together—once skipping to a window curtain and draping it about her coyly in the manner of a model. But simply to gaze on the naked perfections of this little creature—what joy!

Once we went on an overnight trip to Cortina. Coming back, the swerving and rolling of the bus on the narrow Dolomite roads made her sick, and her vomiting started the other passengers off too. She consumed half my brandy flask as she reclined full length on a back seat, moaning like a child.

She had no great opinion of my business ability. When I was faced with a transaction like changing money, she would snap: "Let me talk." There was never any arguing with her. She either couldn't or wouldn't understand. To break away from the few expressions that made up the only communication between us, was to court disaster. Invariably she would mistake my meaning and rage at me or pout. Her favorite expression was "Okay, John," usually spoken sharply whenever I was inclined to scold her.

She insisted it was the first time she had ever consorted with a man. She took for granted that my feelings for her were the same as hers for me. And she proposed to me—very simply and naturally. The difference in our ages mattered not at all. Nor did it matter what her mother and father would say. It only mattered that I was the first and only man she had ever loved.

We parted to meet again in Rome. She would speak to her parents. She would come to my hotel. But she never did. Better so, perhaps. Have not all great love affairs been those that terminated prematurely, before the dreamers wake?

When you are inclined to appraise the future, reflect that men are fools.

I have reached the conviction I should have no convictions.

One of the greatest mercies God has conferred upon us is inability to peer into the future. For whatever good things we could foresee, they would be far outweighed in our minds by the bad. And what person, no matter how sanguine, would be able to free his thoughts from the date of his death?

Does not the wonder of everything cease when it is explained?

Every man loves to contemplate a brilliant future, every woman a lurid past.

If you wish people to magnify your virtues and see

none of your defects, cloak yourself in a mysterious reserve.

There is nothing in an argument more discomforting than a fact.

Observe how little concerned most of the great writers of the past were with contemporary happenings. Take Shakespeare. He was a politically-minded Englishman, but instead of spending his life taking part in politics or thinking how to resist the Spanish Armada, he was busy writing about love and hate, murders and weddings, children rising up against their father, a husband doubting the fidelity of his wife, an exiled king finding happiness in a forest.

There is no greater art than praising rightly.

There can be no division between a man's private life and his public life. Whatever he does in one must be inevitably reflected in the other.

When a person asks for advice, be sure, more often than not, it is merely approval of something he has already decided.

The best way to win an argument is to show that your antagonist is inconsistent with himself.

Is not a friend one to whom we can open the secret recesses of our heart without fear of ridicule?

Conformity to Nature is our highest duty.

How wonderful it would be if the ship of state were managed like a real ship—navigated by men of scientific training and experience, the crew disciplined to obey, the captain free to chart his course and face storms and difficulties without being harassed by the fears and passions of those in his charge.

My greatest hope for America lies in the reverence with which its people regard the memory of Lincoln, a simple, kind, unpretentious man, whose greatness would be unrecognized in many countries.

Observe the folly of the man in Chicago who thought all he had to do to found a movement like Christianity was to have himself crucified.

Distrust the spectacular. It is invariably the effect of a craving for show at the expense of efficiency. Scientific and military expeditions that are well-planned achieve their objectives quickly and smartly, without the blunders and calls for heroic exertion that dramatize ill-prepared enterprises.

Seeing things as they are, untainted by emotion or remembrance or hope,—that is the supreme aim of philosophic living.

Observe how dreaded events are made endurable by contrast to worse possibilities. So death is preferred to lingering illness, war to loss of liberty.

If it were possible for a boy to spring to manhood on an uninhabited island, without sight or knowledge of

women, he would be still possessed with the image of
something strange and beautiful for which all his being
yearned. His failure to define his feelings—to describe
minutely the mysterious phantom on which his happiness
depended—would not disprove its existence. So it is with
our conception of God. We do not see Him; we cannot
define Him; yet we are conscious of a power, greater
than ourselves, to which all our thoughts and hopes are
irresistibly drawn. Is not this greater proof of divine
omnipotence, and life hereafter, than all the labored
dissertations of theology or science?

The art of living is so to control our emotions as
never to be dismayed, never to be overjoyed.

Americans always have a tendency to reject the
obvious.

Difficulties exist only in the mind.

It is a curious fact that, in the licentious 18th Century,
the three figures who were revered most in England
were men of outstanding morality—George III, Pitt the
younger and Samuel Johnson. The influence each wielded
was far in excess of that wielded by men of greater
talents but weaker principles.

We never cease being children. We are only more
skilled at disguising our feelings.

A man who is a hundred years ahead of his time is
just as much of a nincompoop as one a hundred years
behind.

We are possessed sometimes with a desire to have lived in distant times, to have enjoyed the enchantment of the Elizabethan age, for instance; but is it altogether certain that, had we lived as a contemporary of Shakespeare, we would have known Shakespeare or his works? Is not the best of every age laid before us now, for our unalloyed pleasure and instruction, free from the dangers and petty discomforts that went with living in those times?

What is the first duty of a state? The protection, of course, of its own men, women and children, the protection of the sick, the protection of homes, the protection of liberty; and all this is trampled on when a country goes deliberately to war.

It is our mistakes that are remembered, not our achievements.

What happens when people are always leftwing or always rightwing, irrespective of the merits of a question? Why, they go round in circles!

Often the only way a person can be extremely clever is by being extremely wrong.

In dealing with a problem, it is more important to bring out what has been said or done about it in the past, rather than parade forth an array of reasoning and speculation drawn from a view of it in the present. It is silly to spend a lot of time working out new theories and remedies when the past can produce better.

Wisdom never raised any man to eminence. It is too

apt to antagonize people than to captivate them. Those distinguished for wisdom were born to glory like Solomon or owed their elevation to other reasons like Lincoln.

Today the question is not whether a thing is right or wrong but "can we get away with it?"

When you make an important decision in a matter involving future difficulties and are ready to carry through regardless of them, many of these difficulties perforce disappear.

We should have the courage to speak a great deal of seeming nonsense. We are too prone to utter thoughts only when they have been sufficiently matured to go forth into the world without ridicule. Or we echo the thoughts of others that we know have attained a certain respectability. Away with this silliness!

Today, if a man builds a better mouse-trap, the world will beat a path to his door only if he ballyhoos it.

It stands in the village churchyard of Pirbright—a huge, rough monolith inscribed to Bula Matari, breaker of rocks. Its only epitaph—Africa. Poor Henry Stanley! His is the grave not only of a great Englishman but spirits like his who sought vainly to perpetuate a noble work of civilization.

If Stanley's words had been listened to—and those of Livingstone, of Joseph Chamberlain, of Lord Rosebery, —the history of our century would have been different. The vast wealth and energy of the British nation and Empire, the adventurous spirit of their people, would have gone to ridding Africa of inter-tribal war, the slave traffic, disease and famine.

Instead of an England impoverished by two great wars, we should have seen a whole new continent turned into a flowering paradise, with vast areas brought under cultivation and millions of people given the benefits of religion, education and independence. All this could have been achieved for a fraction of the cost in human life and treasure that the British have spent in taking part in the age-old quarrels of Europe. In a sad day for her destiny, she turned, in 1914, to the leadership of war-minded men who, under a veneer of patriotism, had no more her interests at heart than those of France, the country for which they professed so much solicitude.

Ridiculed in his lifetime and remembered by posterity only for the gentlemanly words he spoke on finding Livingstone, Stanley rests in a lonely graveyard instead of beside Livingstone in Westminster Abbey, the grave he coveted. The national rot had set in before he died in 1904, the fatal year of the Entente. "I have done all my work—I have circumnavigated," were among his last words. Only Schweitzer, a German, had the courage and vision of Livingstone and Stanley. Their own nation betrayed them.

Observe the point in human affairs where foresight and preparation can do no more, where we face the unforeseeable, and where we can do nothing except meet it with faith.

A man must always obey the emotions within him to fulfill his proper destiny.

Is it not ironic that much of our study of philosophy

brings us to a state of apathy and fearlessness belonging to the stupid?

———————

There never was a time when there was so little morality among people and so much concern for the morality of others.

———————

Encompassed as all of us are by God's riches, how can the poorest of us complain?

———————

Is it not the certainty of tomorrow that sustains us when night comes? Is it not the remembrance of spring that gladdens our hearts in winter? Why should we despair, then, at death?

———————

Do not many things look forbidding when viewed from a distance?—the woods so thick it would seem impossible to penetrate them, a mountain too precipitous to be climbed, a shore too rockbound to approach; but always when we get closer a way opens before us. And so it is with the problems of life.

———————

True humor comes from a certain recklessness, of not minding what people think.

———————

I have reached the age where I can safely acquire eccentricities without being thought eccentric.

———————

In childhood, religious belief must be supported by certitudes, which through life are dismantled like scaffolding, till a more beautiful structure of doubt and wisdom emerges.

Instead of inspiring men to great deeds, women nowadays are too eager to perform them.

It is more excusable to grieve at someone's birth than at someone's death. Think of all that would give us sorrow if a man's future were unfolded at his birth.

There are many things that make a person amusing, and even ridiculous, to others, which he is forever on his guard to conceal. But these may be the qualities that make him lovable and human. It would be far better, especially if he is a writer, to confess them. See how it was with Chesterfield and Samuel Johnson. Each did his utmost, in writing for the public, to give an impression of great respectability and dignity. Yet both are best remembered for traits or opinions they dared only exhibit in private.

Everything is apparently free until you look closer and perceive it has an orbit, beyond which it cannot go.

In many things of this world, especially great works of art that convey no special meaning to us, we must bow to majority opinion, knowing it is true.

When life is harmonious, people express themselves harmoniously, in music, painting, literature, speech.

Does not good embrace God?

Some men like to win without wooing; some women to be wooed and never won.

Idealization of a woman is like a form of striptease. You clothe your beloved with an array of glittering virtues, which one by one fall away until she is left utterly naked—perchance still beautiful, but more often, alas, plump and ugly.

The great utility of sexual indulgence is that it allows the mind to dwell on worthier things—like a person who ceases to crave for food when his hunger is satisfied.

I am only easy with a woman to whom I can pay compliments.

Memory is our chief source of happiness. The great art of life is to fill the gallery of the mind with beautiful pictures.

There is far more danger in this world from messpots than despots.

Next to the horror of doing things I don't want to do is placing other people in the same dilemma.

Always have enough leisure to pursue the unexpected.

What new monsters are statesmen in their folly conjuring up, from which later, with sublime oratory, they will undertake to save the world?

I always go to a cocktail party as if going into hospital, sorry for myself, hoping for the best and determined to get out as fast as I can. I have heard cocktail

parties referred to as the greatest contribution Americans
have made to the art of living. I wish they had stuck to
hot dogs and Coca Cola. These you can take or leave
alone. But cocktail parties—well, one is bound to be
caught up with two or three in the year out of sheer
inability to think of an excuse, or from an idiotic notion
of talking to someone you have long desired to meet or
haven't seen in a long time. The truth is, I have never
made a lasting friendship at any of these affairs.

You arrive at one and are immediately swept into a
roomful of chattering creatures, all standing about clutching glasses, munching peanuts and looking vastly amused.
Those you are least interested in you converse with most,
and those who appear the most interesting you never
get round to meeting. I suppose there is an art in de-
taching yourself from one group and tacking yourself
onto another. But I never learned it. What terribly dull
topics of conversation prevail! It is a case of sparring
for something of greater interest to talk about, but the
moment you hit upon it there is an interruption, more
introductions follow, and conversation is back where you
started.

Why are cocktail parties tolerated? Are they not de-
signed principally to satisfy the vanity of the giver than
the pleasure of the guests? If conviviality is what is
looked for, it could be achieved more effectively, and at
far less expense, by a small dinner party, at which a
clever host or hostess could take a hand in directing the
conversation. But even under the best conditions, can
one imagine anything to compare with the intelligent
discussions that a Ninon or a Madame Geoffrin used to
preside over in a French salon? Writes Lytton Strachey
of the gatherings at Madame du Deffand's: "Each individual was expected to practise, and did in fact practise
to a consummate degree, those difficult arts which make
the wheels of human intercourse run smoothly—the arts

of tact and temper, of frankness and sympathy, of delicate compliment and exquisite self-abnegation—with the result that a condition of living was produced which, in all its superficial and obvious qualities, was one of unparalleled amenity."

Cocktail parties are a reflection of our times, when art, refinement and delicacy have been smothered by numerical mass.

Our morality today is the very antithesis of Christianity, seeing everything wrong with our neighbors, nothing with ourselves.

The example England set by neutrality during the 19th Century was more effective to the well-being of the world than all her intervention in foreign quarrels thereafter. To call her forbearance isolationism is nonsense. She was responsible for the peace of an overseas empire more extensive than any in history; and to fail in that duty, as she did finally, was to engulf the whole world in war.

Everything done well tends to boredom.

If we do not show mercy to helpless creatures that come within our power, how can we expect God to show mercy to us?

Remember that nations act contrary to their self-interest as often as individuals.

A man who professes to care for a woman belies it by marrying her.

No matter how right we think something is, we must always look to its effect on others. This is not to say we should govern ourselves by the opinions of others. Nothing would be more unprincipled or cowardly. If it is right and nobody will suffer thereby, go ahead and do it in spite of consequences. But if those consequences bring unhappiness to ourselves or others, if no good is achieved, it is wise to hesitate. The right act at the wrong time can be tragic.

Remember that, no matter how well informed we are, we must always act from incomplete evidence.

Learning without curiosity is not learning at all.

The idealist is praised for the difficulty of his life. What nonsense! He goes through life earning the plaudits of the multitude merely by closing his eyes to vexing realities, and mouthing pious platitudes.

There is the same yearning in all of us for immortality as for food, drink and air. And God, in each of these, has not implanted the desire without the fulfillment.

The secret of right living is never to let contemporary life, with all its pressing problems, swamp and master our thinking, but always to illuminate our thoughts by glimpses into the past.

What I find lacking in the paintings in the Academy at Venice is a warm, human quality. There is great richness of color, great nobility in faces and figures, great skill in execution; but we look in vain for emotion, for something to make us feel a certain kinship or sympathy for the people represented. Even in the famous picture of Paul Veronese, *The Banquet in the House of Levi,* there is nothing to make us feel we should like to join the feast. In *The Dream of St. Ursula,* despite the praise lavished on it by John Ruskin, there is nothing that would make us feel like meeting Ursula. Look at the bed-clothes—not a wrinkle in them! This is not the way young ladies sleep when they dream. Where are the garments she has taken off? No girl, no matter how saintly, leaves a room as tidy as this. It is only in the portraits of some nobles that we catch a spark of human feeling. I liked an old man done by Tintoretto. His eyes plainly show he is on the point of death. But the master has made him live forever.

When fear takes possession of the human heart, then farewell common sense, tolerance, decency.

How many people go through life scoffing at faith, forgetting how often they entrust themselves to unknown protectors every time they travel? Why should they not, then, entrust themselves to God?

We lose so much by assuming so much.

Truth nowadays is moulded by men like child's clay—they make anything of it they please.

Cheerfulness is the highest kind of tribute to God.

In childhood one is fearful that spirits exist; in maturity that they don't.

So many situations in life that trouble us should never be treated seriously, but laughed off or forgotten.

One great difference between the wicked and the respectable is that the respectable take longer to discover plausible reasons for the mischief they do.

It is beauty that inspires my love for all things; and it would be as foolish to restrict my devotion to one person as to expect that, on viewing Niagara, I should vow never to behold the Alps.

No man has been venerated so much as Christ; no man has been emulated less.

The fashion of the times is marvelling over things that cannot be understood.

What I find unforgivable in people is rudeness. Courtesy is such a simple commodity that everyone can afford it. I fear I exaggerate courtesy so much that even when I meet it in an undoubted rogue I am charmed.

One's happiness should be like wealth—spread out as much as possible, never apportioned solely to one person or place.

The heroes of mythology have one great lesson to teach us—their readiness to engage in adventures no matter how hazardous or hopeless, trusting to the gods to extricate them.

It is impossible for one person to absorb all the

knowledge of mankind. I become progressively ignorant as the world grows more enlightened.

———

The greatest of faults is not overlooking any in others.

———

Prayer, if nothing else, puts us into an attitude of humility, making us recognize a power above ourselves and bestowing on us a mood of calmness, essential to right thinking.

———

The greatest courage is the courage to act decently.

———

The success of a man in seducing women is one of the least praiseworthy of his accomplishments. Many motives enter into a woman's submission apart from the man—loneliness, vanity, cupidity, a yearning for excitement, a desire for security. It is amazing, in fact, considering such compulsions, that a man must exert himself at all.

———

Be thankful you are still young enough to act the fool.

———

There is more in me of Horatio than of Hamlet—a philosopher unwilling to plunge too deeply into life either through common sense or cowardice, given more to friendship than to love, indifferent equally to good fortune and adversity. But, alas, the Hamlets are those remembered and honored.

———

When one ceases to worry, he ceases to live.

———

To modify a saying of Anglican Archbishop Whately

about God, it makes all the difference in the world whether we put peace in the first place or in the second. Nothing can thrive without peace—neither truth nor liberty, religion nor culture, prosperity nor security; no, nor science either, for it would destroy itself in the end.

When one is deterred by difficulties, he is indifferent to what he seeks.

Remember that what appears common sense to one is folly to another.

The surest mark of a genius is his ability to absorb everything that interests him, without straining his powers of observation or memory; so that he seems to have come by his knowledge by instinct. What is laborious to others is easy and natural to him. Everyone is a genius if he will only acknowledge the thing that comes pleasurably to him, no matter how small or unworthy it might appear.

People get something from going to church if only in putting on their best clothes and manners, in being pleasant to their neighbors, and not talking for a while.

The tall funnel of an outbound freighter, directly ahead of our ferryboat as we left Manhattan, set me musing all the way across the harbor. The funnel was banded black-white-red-white-black, the colors of Liverpool's old Harrison Line. What a thrill it used to be as a boy seeing one of these ships steaming out of the estuary of the Mersey. There would be a cry on my street, "Hurry, one of your dad's ships is going out!"

And off all of us would dash to the shore to see which one it was.

What fascinating names they had—the *Wayfarer,* the *Explorer,* the *Wanderer,* the *Magician,* the *Author.* I swear I got an ambition to be an author from gazing on this last favorite, off perhaps to East Africa, and hearing my father tell tales of "Captain Arthur of the *Author.*" And of "Mad Billy" Brown of the *Dictator,* who went to prison for killing a lascar in Calcutta, once tried to murder his wife at sea, and drowned finally when his ship was in a collision in the Mersey.

What unforgettable moments they were when my father would take me to one of Harrison's sailings and I would sit gazing with awe at the captain while my father sat "having a nip" with him in his cabin and waiting for the pilot. Then I would stand with my father on the dock while the vessel went out through a set of locks into the river, the crew clustered on deck never knowing whether they would return. Half the fleet were torpedoed in the war then raging.

Once, when a cluster of Harrison funnels peeped above the sheds of distant Seaforth amid four-funnelers like the *Olympic* and *Aquitania,* I started off along the shore to get a closer look and became lost and had the whole street out looking for me after dark.

What a crowd of memories can be stirred up by a little thing! A black-white-red-white-black funnel!

———

One of the loveliest aspects of life when I first knew America was the front-porch. It brought the whole family together in the cool of the evening. Neighbors dropped in or stopped for a chat. There was music and singing and laughter. There was gossiping, too, for nobody could step out or receive a visitor without the entire neighborhood knowing it. Now Americans cannot be bothered to sit on front-porches and watch life as it passes. They're too busy watching it inside on television.

I love Corot's paintings of forest scenes. They make you feel you are lost amid all the splendor of greenery, puzzled how you will ever get out. Hobbema has this same intimacy. Both masters impart to the spectator the sense of being there. The admiration you feel for other painters gives way, in them, to an appreciation of the scene itself. It is like the best writing—you are not aware of the writer because you are too absorbed in what he is saying.

My life ceases to have meaning without leisure to read and reflect.

Flexibility is the essence of wisdom. Never take up a rigid position that later, through altered circumstances, you are not ready to abandon. There is a time to advance, to retreat; a time to resist, to surrender.

Sun-worshippers are not found among people accustomed to the sun.

Is it not curious that the Swiss, with all their years of freedom and peace, so conducive to reflection and genius, have produced so few great men? Those like Calvin, Voltaire and Gibbon, whose names are indelibly associated with Switzerland, were born and nurtured elsewhere. There is something in the Swiss character that makes for tidiness and order. Their sanity in a world of noise and confusion is refreshing. Their manners and intelligence are beyond all praise. Yet what is missing is a restless discontent—a striving for things outside their grasp, outside all reason, which, while producing temporary disorder and unhappiness, also creates the conditions out of which progress comes.

Opportunities, like life itself, are always imperfect. Take them when they come.

How few of us appreciate monotony! It is the by-product of precision and efficiency. It is the bogey of little minds that crave excitement, generally at the expense of worthier creatures who ask only for tranquillity. See how it is with flying. How much preferable is monotony in flying than excitement!

Remember that nothing is ever perfect in this imperfect world.

The trouble about putting yourself in the other person's place is that you forget you are not the same person. Instead of doing as he might wish, you may act completely at variance with him. You have your whims, foibles, opinions, prejudices, ideas, that are possibly contrary to his.

Be firm in this resolve—never build up treasures on earth that the fear of losing them will make you miserable or deter you from doing what is right.

The extent of the resources that always lie at hand is surprising to one who will pause to look for them and not be engrossed in looking for distant succor.

We should learn this lesson from nature—it seldom does anything in a hurry.

Do not be deceived into depreciating something simple you have done. Common sense is always simple.

Unhappy is the man who puts himself at the mercy of one woman!

Why do we look upon the Venus de Milo as perfect? A perfect body perhaps. But is that all there is to perfection? Are we to model ourselves only on the outward beauties, not on those of the mind or spirit? Look at all these pretty girls gazing so enviously on Venus. Are they not more lovely, more exciting?

Many people believe that because they can supply a reason for doing something questionable, then that, perforce, makes it right.

One must always strive for order in his life. Is this not the attribute of the universe?

I found at St. Peter's, Rome, a new sense of the truth of Christianity. But it was not in the cathedral itself—not before the magnificent altar where so much dogma has been proclaimed and so much pageantry enacted—but far below in the old Roman street where Peter and other early Christians were buried. Here was the down-to-earthiness we seek so much in religion! If only archaeologists could dig out as easily the falseness and vanity that have entombed this gentlest, kindest, most revolutionary of all religions!

I have sympathy and respect for one of the first Christians, Marcion, who tried to establish Christianity as a completely new religion by compiling a Christian Bible, purged of the Old Testament. It omitted Luke's

account of Christ's birth, which was plainly a belated
and futile attempt to convert the Jewish nation by de-
picting Jesus as the messiah forecast by their prophets.
But the Roman Church rejected it.

The damage that the Old Testament has done to pure
Christianity has been incalculable. The right to commit
all the crimes under heaven—murder, massacre, treachery, war,—have been derived from a scrupulous reading
of these scriptures. They are, strictly speaking, the history of a simple, God-minded people. That such a history—or any history—should serve as a code of conduct,
with passages taken from their context and invested with
mysterious oracular power, is preposterous. It would
have been far better for humanity if these books had been
neglected and forgotten than to have been fastened on
for centuries by ignorance and bigotry. Yet this would
have meant losing a rich cultural and religious heritage.
Read properly, the Old Testament is a tremendous force
for good in the world. Interpreted fanatically, it becomes
an incentive to evil and hypocrisy. The bloodiest deeds
of Christianity must be ascribed to the Old Testament.

But how can Christianity be separated from it? Read
through the Gospels and one is astounded by the multi-
farious references to Abraham, Isaac, Jacob, Moses,
Elijah, Isaiah, Jonah, and other early Biblical figures.
Christ's whole thought was fashioned and colored by
the study of them. To keep the law of Moses was one
of the most frequent and passionate of his entreaties.

Yet Christ went further. He built upon this venerable
foundation a creed of vast utility and beauty, never
known or preached before in the world. He preached
the religion of the heart, of joyousness in Nature and
friendship, of freedom from the narrowness, the rigid-
ity, the self-righteousness of a dominating priesthood.
Above all, Christ himself stands above what he has said
and what has been written about him, a figure of nobility

and perfection, the closer to whom we come the better for all of us. That he has survived the inhumanities committed in his name is a measure of his greatness. I shall go further—I cannot think that a mere historical figure, no matter how excellent, could have achieved all that Christ has done without the attributes of a god. Even when allowance is made for the undoubted mistakes and misrepresentations of his disciples in their record of him, enough comes through to demonstrate his divinity.

———

Persons who are actuated by bad motives are always ready to ascribe them to others.

———

It is necessary in writing to have the theme always in view—a theme attractive enough to keep us driving through a multitude of petty difficulties, a theme precise enough to prevent digressions; for it is in writing as it is in travelling—faster progress can be made if we know exactly where we are going.

———

Life can be exciting to him who sees it as an adventure.

———

Many things assume an importance in telling that they didn't have in happening.

———

Some persons you must knock down before they look up to you.

———

It is much better for a person to come round to a truth himself than to have it thrust upon him.

———

Materialists scoff at the idea of walking on water.

But behold, Nature, at 32 degrees fahrenheit, unfolds the miracle!

Never regulate your life by fear.

How can a man govern a country who has not learned to govern himself?

Always have an objective, near or remote, substantial or illusory, that calls forth your enthusiasm. For without enthusiasm, all exertion is labor.

All these thousands of dead reposing in the cemetery in which I walk proclaim to me in one voice: "Thou art alive! Use thy life with all gentleness and usefulness, whilst thou may!"

The truth that we must be forever remembering is that many things are neither right nor wrong, good nor bad, but are merely what their nature makes them; and it is for us either to accept them or leave them alone.

Nature is a stern taskmaster and requires that we meet her dictates promptly and well; but how fortunate we are that, in so many of them, pleasure is the manner of it!

When life ceases to be a worry, it ceases to be life.

Learn to distinguish between selfishness and selfhood. The first embraces all that is reprehensible, the other everything that is good. Selfhood is akin to sainthood, because it recognizes the divinity within ourselves.

Every distortion of truth is fatal to the distortioner.

Does not the life of the universe consist in the circulation of the heavenly bodies? The life of a human being in the circulation of blood? The life of Nature in the circulation of seasons? The life of rivers in the circulation of vapor? Would it not be easy, in watching water pouring over a cataract, to think that is the last of it? As it would be to watch a receding comet and think it is the last of that? Or to look upon a tree in autumn and think it will never bloom again? Yet, throughout the universe, there is this continual rise and fall, coming and going, appearing and disappearing. May this not be the secret of our existence?—that the soul, or life force, goes forth from the body at death to join the eternal rotation?

The women most worthy of our esteem are not those who make us love them as make us more happy with ourselves.

It would have been as difficult for a man 500 years ago to understand the miracles of the first century as those of the twentieth. If his credulity was strained at reading how a cripple stood up and walked, consider how incredulous he would have been at hearing how a person could talk with another across the ocean or see what people were doing in another part of the country or how a person could speed to a distant part of the world in a few hours.

Keats has noted how Fortune deserts him who woos her too assiduously. The reason is clear. One intent on fame is too often striving after qualities that are foreign to himself. When, in disgust, he gives up the struggle and falls back on himself, his chances of success are greater.

Government today has evolved into a simple formula —in foreign affairs raise hell, in wartime raise men, in a financial squeeze raise taxes.

What I regret most in life are lost opportunities—the trivial, perhaps, more than any, because they were easier to grasp.

I never worry what my rivals are doing. I am always too intent on trying to do the right thing myself.

Never let a false regard for custom or decorum keep you from making life an exciting adventure. Remember that what distinguishes us from the men and women who have preceded us is life. Enjoy it to the full. Drink deeply of it like a traveller of water going into an unknown desert. Give thanks to God that we still have life and the capacity to enjoy it. Learn as much as we can. Bring joy to others and never consciously hurt anyone. Fulfill the law of our being.

Our rulers are like the crazy youth in South Africa who got a plane into the air without the slightest knowledge of how to fly, then had to drop a frantic note asking how to land it.

Life is harder for a woman today. Thirty or more

years ago she could light up a cigarette and have the satisfaction of being regarded as wicked without the bother of proving it.

The motto "Let George do it" is fine if George can do it better.

We should not go through life believing that, because we think and act differently than before, we must be right now and wrong then. It is not a question of right, only of change.

To rebel against life is as foolish as rebelling against a game. The rules are not ours; we may not approve them; we may think the referee is unfair. But once we are in the game we must see it through like good sportsmen.

There are some persons who love to be secretive about their lives for the reason, I suppose, there is nothing to be secretive about.

The only other person I ever knew who succeeded, like me, in reading through Lord Morley's *Life of Gladstone* was Helen Keller. "Is it not ponderous?" I remember her asking me one evening aboard the French liner *Champlain*. Yet it was hailed at the beginning of the century as one of the greatest biographies since Boswell. The reason it is so boring, I think, is that Morley drew a line between Gladstone's public life and his private one, and we are treated to none of the intimate touches that would bring him to life as a person. It is the kind of biography that appeals vastly to the family of the subject, but to no one else. Gladstone is presented in such perfect colors that we are rendered suspicious. We see him seldom behind the scenes. We get only the picture of the statesman and orator that was known to millions of his contemporaries.

There is one chapter of Morley and Gladstone going together to Biarritz, when we are permitted to see the great Liberal in moments of relaxation, and are furnished with specimens of his informal talk. But this occurs after an interminable history of the Home Rule struggle for Ireland, which has but little interest to the reader today. There is little to suggest the strained relationship between Gladstone and Victoria. Indeed, from Morley's account, we would gather these two were in perfect harmony; whereas we know from other sources, particularly the letters of Henry Ponsonby, the Queen's private secretary, that Victoria detested Gladstone and did everything in her power to thwart him. Yet the old man never seemed to perceive her true feelings for him, which makes one distrust his powers of discernment in other matters. He was hesitant at breaking the news of his retirement to her for fear it would subject her to a stroke! When he did, she replied coldly that she was glad he was retiring *at his age.*

She who had suffered so much constitutionally under his ministries made him smart with one final stroke of power, which was, at the same time, quite constitutional —she never consulted him about his successor when he was ready to recommend a non-entity, Lord Spencer, and took as her Prime Minister one of the wisest men of his time, the scholarly, handsome Lord Rosebery.

When the outlook is dark, take a shortened view of what lies ahead—like a driver on a road that is winding and rough.

The strongest links to those we love, living or dead, are little fleeting recollections.

I am supremely happy when I have the time and money to buy books, supremely unhappy when I want leisure to read them.

The great aim of living is to elevate oneself above everything that limits the spirit—race, religion, class, money, work.

The folly of others is not sufficient to excuse the folly of ourselves.

Many people worship difficulties like divinities.

The anticipation of seeing my favorite places confers on me as much pleasure as seeing them.

What the world needs is God-natured men.

With most of us, removal of one worry merely makes way for another.

It is always the Alexanders, the Caesars and Napoleons who draw man's highest praise. How foolish! They have attained success by trampling on the rights of humanity. Those who deserve our admiration have mastered the supreme art of elevating themselves by serving others.

It is wise, when baffled by a problem, to move slowly, confident that, with patience and watchfulness, something will arise to remedy it.

Far worse than a lazy fool is an energetic one.

The essence of love is freedom.

Britain's chief concern should be paying for her previous follies, not incurring others.

Americans have ways of circumventing common sense that are astonishing to other nations.

One can only prepare for the future by doing what is right in the present.

The English girl I was with when I visited the Chateau of Montaigne, in the quiet Bordeaux countryside, preferred to stay outside and "get the sun." Her exposure to Montaigne might have been more salutary. Indeed, I scarcely know of an English person of "proper" middle-class upbringing, taught to distrust his or her impulses, who would not benefit from a reading of a man who said he would willingly return from the dead "to give the lie to anyone who portrayed me other than I was, even though it were to honor me."

Montaigne was Thackeray's bedside book, and perhaps Shakespeare's,—two Englishmen who learned never to be afraid of expressing emotion.

Here in the Chateau you see Montaigne hurrying across the courtyard to his hideaway tower in the wall, where he escapes from wife, daughter and guests to play with his cat or to gaze out on his farmyard or, more importantly, spy on himself, the object of his everlasting attention. A chapel was on the first floor, a bedroom on the second and his study and library on the third; and here one can still see Greek and Latin quotations on the beams, as this from Terence: *"Homo sum, humani a me nil alienum puto"* (I am a man; I consider nothing human alien to me).

Hour after hour he sits in his tower writing his essays while the noisy world of Catherine of Medici and Henry of Navarre rages in endless war about him. Once a commotion at the gate—it is open to friend or enemy— brings him down in haste, and in the courtyard he encounters an exhausted rider who gasps he has ridden away from an ambush with his men and craves shelter. Presently the stranger is joined by four or five other horsemen, then more and more, until thirty armed men pack the courtyard; and too late the castle wakens to its danger. But Montaigne continues to play the frank and friendly host, serving refreshments to all, inviting them inside to rest, chatting with them; and at last the leader, ashamed of his treachery, remounts and gallops away with his downcast company.

What an egotist this man Montaigne is! Endlessly talking about himself, his reaction to danger, his pleasures, his habits, his lovemaking, his pains, his thoughts. With anyone else, this might be boring and nauseating; but with Montaigne—how delightful! To pick up his essays is to listen to one of the most entertaining, profound and genial souls who ever lived. We enrich our own life by imbibing the wisdom of this other. Why do we find so many things to complain about? We should complain, says Montaigne, only at things that fail to conform to what is natural in themselves. For the conceit that we must fear is not the conceit of Montaigne's but the conceit that makes us expect the whole world to bow to ourselves.

When you face a seemingly hopeless problem, probe for a few more facts, and, behold, the problem vanishes.

The secret of success is to guard against rigid attitudes, so that the mind and heart can be open always to what is right.

Some people read nothing but the Bible, as though God stopped speaking to men after it was written.

The sight which is most pleasing to me is the one which excites the most thought.

Ignorant people always adore what they cannot understand.

Nations have the choice of thinking historically or thinking hysterically—the long perspective against an obsessive moment of doubt, fear and panic.

The less one knows of his neighbors the better one likes them.

I reject the notion that the old year stands for nothing but bad and the new year nothing but good. There is always too much thankfulness in my heart to rejoice in the passing of the old year.

Kings have been deposed in Europe only to be replaced by Everyman, equally despotic.

Our lives are governed more and more by miscreants, from whom society seeks to protect itself with a set of restraints that penalize the decent.

How many opportunities are lost by the lament, "I haven't the time!"

The secret of joyful living is to attain freedom from everything that confines the soul—from fear, from envy, from jealousy, from covetousness, from evil habits, from excess of all kinds.

How easy it is to regress when we think we are moving forward! A few imperceptible turns—those slight deviations "which don't matter"—and, lo, we are circling back where we started!

There are some situations we hate to be thought responsible for, but don't mind profiting from.

I write a letter, and next day read it over with trepidation, wondering how much I may have changed and how much of it I will now repudiate.

Take away the clutter of foolishness that stands in the way of common sense—the jealousies, vanities and artificialities that surround us like germs—and life can be pleasant and useful.

It is a commentary of our time that, when one hears laughter, he doesn't imagine it emanates from an excess of joy, but from malice or ridicule.

How hateful are those people who feel they cannot raise their own importance except by running down that of others!

There is no sadder book in all the world than one's own address book, a record of love and friendship, doomed in so short a time to become dark with deletions.

One who lives much in the past, as I do, must inevitably miss much in the present.

As I grow older, I become more impatient with people, but only because people become more impatient themselves, with no time for pleasantness or courtesy.

The greatest joy is to dwell in one's own mind free of care or distraction.

The closer we come to Nature the closer we come to God.

It is possible for friendship to attain such perfection that personal contact is superfluous, with all its hazard of misunderstanding and boredom.

Too many of our political leaders have lawyer minds —the propensity to make the best possible case for any issue, no matter how bad.

Talk is the enemy of action.

A man is wise to listen to a woman, foolish to heed her.

We may see a landscape, attend a play, meet a person, and not be conscious of any pleasure until long after, when it bubbles into our being like a tune we have carried subconsciously from the theatre.

The less restrained we are, the more we tend to be happy. But, alas, we are under restraint all our lives, from the discipline of school to the infirmities of age.

Those women are supreme who make us know and love ourselves.

So many actions that are suspected of being malicious are ascribable only to stupidity.

It is the nature of man to make the best of bad situations. But to step purposely into them is madness.

There are some places, some friends, some books, some paintings that one never gets to know perfectly. They attract and puzzle us eternally. It is a joy to come back to them, to gaze on them again, to think finally we have drawn from them everything that interests us, only to know, ultimately, we haven't. There is always a newness about them, and always mystery.

The only Englishman, I think, who can be compared

with Lincoln in wisdom and simplicity is Richard Cobden, who more than any other person in political life
under Victoria made Parliament and the country respon-
sive to reason and common sense. I love the story told
of Sir Robert Peel, the Prime Minister, listening to one
of Cobden's great Corn Law speeches and taking copious
notes to refute him. Finally he tore them up. "You
answer him," said Peel, turning to the cabinet minister
next to him; "I can't."

Cobden was one of the few men who could change
votes in the House of Commons, and he did it not by
passion but by an irresistible flow of quiet logic. His
voice was continually raised for peace, reduction of
armaments, Parliamentary reform, fiscal sanity, and a
system of national education. He was such an admirer
of American democracy that he and his great ally, John
Bright, used to be referred to in Parliament, not always
flatteringly, as "the members for the United States."
He hated pomp, declined public honors and refused to
join the cabinet of Palmerston because he distrusted his
policy of intervention everywhere in the world. "The
world never knew so warlike and aggressive a people as
the British," he complained once. And he did his utmost
to divert that spirit constructively to other fields.

There was no one who more recognized the distinction
between the economic life of a nation and its diplomatic
life than Cobden. His formula was to internationalize
the first and to circumscribe the second, allowing his
country to trade with all the world while trying to fix
its attention on problems at home rather than those
abroad. Confounding the economic and diplomatic areas
of national activity, either by isolating both or inter-
nationalizing both, is one of the causes of the world's
unrest.

I heard of a woman bookkeeper in a luggage firm who
dispensed salary increases to her fellow employees with-

out the knowledge of her boss, wrecked his business and drove him to suicide. How often are generous actions, uncontrolled by reason, pregnant of disaster.

A fabulous memory often deceives people into thinking they have met with a brilliant mind. The contrary may be true. Charlotte Addison, the daughter of Joseph Addison, could recite every line of poetry her father wrote—a total of more than one million words! Yet she was so feeble-minded she could not write a coherent sentence.

Too many Presidents imitate Lincoln, delighting to agonize over problems while shuffling, I suppose, about their living quarters in slippers and dressing gown, shoulders hunched and glancing from time to time at the Bible. Usually the decision, when it comes, is a horrifying one. With British Prime Ministers the matter is worse. They have no model, or if they do their choice goes back no further than Churchill. Now the model I recommend is Harun al-Rashid, who would go about the bazaars of Baghdad as a merchant, listening to his people and getting down to problems of everyday living. I admit, however, I cannot see Mr. Nixon or Mr. Heath following this excellent practice without the accompaniment of Secret Service agents and photographers. Churchill was in the London underground only once. Then he got lost. Such is the fate, alas, of all our leaders when they try to get close to the people.

A country run by a majority can often be as fatally misruled as a school run by its children.

The trouble with a middle-of-the-road policy is that you are liable to be hit by traffic both ways.

The way to be liked by fools is to be one.

A re-appraisal of Winston Churchill is desperately needed today. It is not a case of debunking. It is a case of setting the man into proper perspective before a dangerous, Napoleon-like myth grows up around him.

Like Napoleon, whom he idolized, Churchill was actuated by a craving for excitement, a thirst for military glory. Whatever conflicting forces were present in his character—and it was a complex one—this was uppermost. It was manifest in everything he did—from a boy playing with hundreds of toy soldiers, to a youth spreading a map of the world on the floor to see where there was a war he could get into, to an officer in India, when he would curse his major for making peace with hostile tribes just when he was looking forward to "a splendid fight."

Writer A. G. Gardiner, an astute observer of Churchill during his first years in Parliament, called him "a soldier first, last, and always,"—a man "not so much concerned about who the enemy may be or about the merits of the quarrel as about being in the thick of the fight and having a good time."

All honor to Churchill for standing forth a figure of defiance to Hitlerism. He had not become His Majesty's first minister, he avowed, to preside over the dissolution of the British Empire. But his prior acts contributed to it. For he was a prime factor with Asquith, Haldane and Sir Edward Grey in his country's involvement in the first world war, with its aftermath of starvation, desperation and misery through Europe, out of which Hitlerism came.

He always saw war as a drama with himself in the principal part—not as a tragedy in which the lives and happiness of millions were at stake. After the 1918 Armistice, when the youth of his country lay slaughtered, he strove to continue the war against Bolshevist Russia, earning the rebuke of an exasperated Prime Minister, Lloyd George, that he would succeed only in driving Britain to revolution and in spreading Communism through an impoverished Europe.

That was the way with Churchill—his voice was forever on the side of force at those times when the alternatives of peace had not been fully explored. Such counsellors are common in the political life of every country. But few have had the fervency and eloquence to make themselves listened to like Churchill.

He was the gambler who staked everything on the game, for the sheer excitement of it. Only what he staked was not what he possessed himself but the resources, the youth, the very life of his country, as well as the future of the Empire for which he professed so much devotion. His later lamentations for his country were like the lamentations of a gambler, who sees his family ruined and prostrate but still overwhelms them with love.

People everywhere preach internationalism and daily become more national.

Whatever problem has been brought about by love must perforce be soluble.

I am prejudiced against all nationalities who cannot rise above themselves.

Each of us should cultivate a detective sense, deducing whole pages of truth from momentary glimpses and fragments of fact.

Are not hours of activity merely a preparation for sleep, the prime condition of man?

I have no use for self-glorified "men of honor." Most of them are rogues. How many seemingly respectable statesmen have sent thousands upon thousands of their countrymen to die in war rather than dishonor a worthless treaty? Herod was a man of honor, executing John the Baptist rather than break his word to a trollop.

Greatness lies principally in foolishness. What genius ever stuck to the rules? Did Christ do the "proper" thing? Or Socrates? Or Joan of Arc?

The old man would wait in a doorway for hours until he saw me approaching, then emerge chuckling at something he had heard or read and wanted to tell me. Impatiently I would disengage myself, pleading I had something urgent to deal with elsewhere. What was this urgency? I have forgotten. But the memory of laughing Bill remains long after all else has faded.

I never try to change people whom I care for, only to make them more happy with themselves.

It is an awful thing in life never to achieve what we have dreamed. But how much worse when we have done so, and are stifled by the reality of it, and find nothing beyond.

It is not death that is tragic—it is life that is unfulfilled.

The art in all things is to expose oneself confidently to facts, then await the impression, like a photographer toiling in a darkroom.

The generality of American women love to be propositioned, not because they derive any particular pleasure from sleeping with men—some of them never do—but because they enjoy having inspired the invitation.

What could better illustrate eternity than the sight of a pregnant woman beside the grave of a parent?

A beautiful, enticing woman is like an itch—wonderful if you can touch her, agonizing if you can't.

The death of all I love, humans or animals, diminishes me in proportion to the love I have lost.

Far better than always being in love is always falling in love.

We imitate what we admire. So let us admire rightly.

Quoting a man against himself may be the height of rudeness, as Samuel Johnson complained, but it is also the height of persuasiveness.

Writing a book is like putting a roast in the oven. It depends on the degree of heat how well it turns out.

Let us face difficulties like a tree that stands the straightest, leaning neither this way nor that, but resistant to the storm from whatever quarter it comes.

Everything beautiful needs time to germinate, either in itself or the assimilative mind.

A strong will coupled with a faulty judgment can be disastrous.

True relaxation comes from losing a sense of hurry.

One can be in communion with God without words.

I am always close to God when I am close to myself.

Follow the ways of Nature except in its ruder manifestations, detectable to common sense.

Decades roll around with the celerity of years as we get older, as though life were saying: "Here now, do what you have to do quickly, and make room for them who follow."

"You're too young, Frieda," a man's voice was saying on the path behind me. "Stay here and read your book." A girl's voice was arguing to accompany the two men— father and brother as it turned out—to the beach farther along. "No," the first voice was telling her gently, "stay here and we'll pick you up in about an hour."

Presently Frieda appeared, threading her way cautiously among the huge rocks until she found one against which she could rest. She was about 16—a shy, pretty, blue-eyed girl clad in sandals, white shorts and a blouse. For several minutes she sat gazing toward another island of the Hyeres. Then she got up, skipped down to the lower rocks and looked toward the nudist beach where her father and brother had gone. It was too far off to see anything. With a timid glance at me, she returned to her book, sat down and took off her shorts and blouse, revealing herself in panties and bra.

She sat like this for several minutes. Then she stood up again, slipped her panties off, unhooked her bra and sat down abruptly. She picked up her book, but she was too busy glancing right and left and back at the path to be reading. Without getting up, she shifted out of the shade of her rock to where the sun was beating down with midday intensity. She enjoyed this for a few minutes, then she rose quickly and skipped down to the water again.

She was beautifully proportioned. Thighs, buttocks, breasts, shoulders and arms flowed together in perfect symmetry. Her tiny, dark triangle of hair accentuated the dazzling whiteness of her body. Conscious, I thought, of my admiring gaze, she leapt from one rock to another looking for a place to swim. I pointed to where a cluster of rocks sloped conveniently to the water. She came over, took the hand I offered to help her across, and gave me a ring and wristwatch to mind. Then she tripped gaily to the water's edge. kicked off her sandals and dived in.

She rose up with a joyous cry, waved to me as I stood watching, and stroked vigorously to a point about a hundred yards off shore. I joined her, and she said it was her first time in the water without a swimsuit. It was glorious, she exclaimed—far better than the bathing at Port-Cros where she, her mother, father and brother were staying. "They're very strict with me," she said. "What if they could see me now!"

Then she swam back, retrieved her ring and wristwatch, dried herself with a towel I offered her, and scrambled naked up the rocks to see if father and brother were returning. A family of picnickers were walking along the path and she smiled at them unembarrassed. A great modern preacher, Dr. Robert J. McCracken, has said: "The body, being sacred, is not something of which there is any need to be ashamed." So it was with Frieda.

She came back to her clothes, dressed quickly, and was chatting with me when there was a shout from the path, "Frieda, hurry. We'll be missing the boat." And off she went with a parting cry, "Goodbye—and thank you."

To possess the means and leisure to absorb knowledge all at once, would be as fatal to our well-being as trying to stuff ourselves with food and drink for a year.

Going to church does not, in itself, make a Christian. Indeed, it may breed a monster of depravity, one who is convinced that, by an outward show of piety, he is incapable of wrong.

Who is the worse nuisance—the child misbehaving or the parent reproving it?

A piece of writing that must be written again and again was doubtless not worth the writing in the first place.

Good intentions mask a multitude of sins.

Never grope for thoughts that do not rise into your consciousness naturally.

In a world gone mad, strive to make your home a citadel of comfort and sanity.

Never undervalue what is cheap and profuse. How eagerly does man cling to water in a desert! How joyfully does he embrace love and goodness and beauty when he is in danger of losing all!

Usually in dealings with other people, we are so concerned with our own difficulties we forget the others have them too.

No man, how ever wealthy, can command all I possess in friends, in books, in thoughts, in a warm and loving home.

Never stake your happiness on the present moment from a feeling "it is all thou hast." It is not. Life should be a compound of the past, the present and the future— the past brimming with joyous memories, the present with agreeable activity, the future with hope.

Mankind has less to fear from the ruthlessness of the cruel than the indifference of the respectable.

It is inevitable that, as the authority of the state increases, the freedom of the individual declines.

What all of us should have to go far in life is a *slight* case of madness.

To hold fast to what is noblest in a nation's life should be the supreme aim of every people.

I go abroad not to get to know people so much as to get to know myself better.

When royalty was all-powerful, the individual counted for nothing. So it is today now that the people are sovereign.

Never despair at your inability to communicate with others. It is far better than being able to communicate, only to differ.

I dreamt of crossing New York Bay in a ferryboat, when a dreadful, indescribable calamity occurred. It seemed that the heavens opened, and people were frozen in horror by a thunderstroke of divine wrath, as though the world was coming to an end. I seemed—how I cannot say—to have attained a position of safety, from which I called to people to join me. One man, still with terror in his face, walked in a daze to me across the water! Oh, dreadful parable! Are unbelievers to know there is a God only when the world has been driven to destruction?

If we allow our minds to dwell on it, there is enough sadness in our lives to sink us.

Beauty in woman can excuse a thousand faults.

If there were no seasons, if earth flowered under a perpetual summer, what mortal could endure the monotony? Even the thought of paradise terrifies us by the promise of eternal joy.

There is no intrinsic merit in many qualities we look upon as good, such as firmness, persistency, kindness, mercy, hope. Some of them, applied at the wrong time or under the wrong circumstances, can be positive evils. The superior man knows when to be firm or yielding, persistent or passive, kind or hard, merciful or just, hopeful or pessimistic. One virtue, persevered in, may lead to irretrievable ruin.

The dog that is tethered is wilder than the one that is free. Freedom breeds friendliness and gentleness.

There is something symbolic in the famous statue of the Winged Victory in the Louvre. It has lost its head!

Are we not closer to God in a forest than in a Cathedral? Are not the hours that we spend contemplating the works of God—in living a sermon—better spent than in listening to one?

None of us would have the courage or heart to go on living if we were acquainted with a millionth part of the cruelty and misery that lie about us.

One should not be so well prepared for something he undertakes—so all-wise, precise and calculating—that he has no room for a little foolhardiness.

Benvenuto Cellini's life of himself is one of the finest autobiographies I have read. Yet I cannot imagine a character I should have less enjoyed meeting. He was vain, arrogant, impatient, unstable, and so quick-tempered that, offended perhaps by something you said, he would have ended by springing at your throat. He would have bored you with his boasting, incensed you with his rudeness. There was no crime, you would have felt, of which he was not capable.

But in his autobiography he commands our interest and sympathy throughout. How explain the paradox? To dissimulation? On this we must agree with his translator, John Addington Symonds, that Cellini never consciously deviates from truth. He composes too rapidly to deceive

the reader. He is so intent upon telling everything that
has happened to himself that he has no time for anyone
else. Popes, cardinals, kings, dukes, and great artists
crowd his pages, but always in subordination to himself.
He never feels compelled to turn aside and tell you something about them that may have puzzled history. "I mean
to treat of those things only which concern myself," he
writes.

His egotism is akin to Casanova's. He also has Casanova's flair for adventure, travel and romance. But he
never dreams of going out of his way to meet a great
person as Casanova did. On a visit to Venice Cellini tells
us nothing about Titian—for the good reason, I suppose,
he never bothered to look him up. And he never dwells
too long over his love affairs. That would have given
more importance to his mistresses than they assumed in
his own mind. He never tarries very long over any incident. He is too eager to proceed to the next. And here, in
the impetuosity of his narrative, is the chief delight of
his book.

Never think the world is run entirely by reason. Be
on your guard against fools.

When you prepare assiduously for the foreseeable difficulties, you will always be ready for those that are unexpected.

I have heard men say of others, in depreciation of
their ability, that they would never burn up the world. Is
this not a kind of compliment? Are not those who burn
up the world the Mussolinis and Hitlers—the braggarts
and showoffs—who make up for their want of common-
sense and decency by wicked subterfuges?

It is a safe assumption that the things we force our memory to retain are not for us. There should be little or no difficulty in remembering everything that is essential to our work if it is what we are best fitted to do.

If one heeded the plane accidents he reads about, he would never fly; all the car accidents, he would never drive; all the accidents to pedestrians, he would never walk.

Sorrow is universal. Those who come to commiserate with us are themselves overtaken by the griefs they seek to dispel.

What is appalling about people today is their disregard for the rights and feelings of others.

You cannot have chivalry without lovely women to be chivalrous about. Say a man today were to throw his coat into the mud for a woman to walk over. She would double over laughing.

In a contest of minds, as in a contest of armies, it is important always to hold something in reserve—to bring matters to a crucial point where your antagonist is wavering, then to introduce all you are holding back in one decisive sweep.

Who am I to mourn for a lost one? Am I immortal?

Beware of too much vigilance against errors. It is inevitable, in the best work, that mistakes must occur.

When they do, make the best of it and push on. Observe the blunders in Shakespeare—lions in a French forest, Hector quoting Aristotle, a seacoast in Bohemia, Cleopatra playing bowls. Some of our perfectionists would reject such works, seeing only the blemishes. The thing to remember is that, if we lived a dozen centuries, we would never be infallible. The energy we expend in guarding against mistakes can be better utilized in getting something done quickly, leaving our shortcomings to the detection of little minds.

It seems a pity that, while other nationalities are concerned with more interesting parts of the human anatomy, the British are obsessed by the stiff upper lip.

Why does the world look upon Romeo and Juliet as the pattern of perfect love? I suppose because they never lived as husband and wife.

Is it not strange that France, the champion of republicanism, should delight in showing the visitor the glories of her kings?

In plotting a fiction story difficult to reconcile to life, reflect how hard it is to explain how we got into strange complications in our own life.

The art of enjoyment is to transform seemingly trifling happenings into pleasurable experiences.

One of the worst failings of men is not foreseeing the consequences of their own acts.

I have no patience with people who undertake something without being able to finish it.

Just as needful as a frequent bathing of the body is a frequent bathing of the spirit.

To be indifferent to most things, one must be ardent about one.

A cat's life is a succession of present moments, unsullied by recollection of the past or fear of the future. So it should be with all of us.

The priest intoned a graveside prayer for the dead, while the nearby brook, more eloquently, proclaimed life eternal.

Another's misdeed must be judged in relation to the sum-total of his acts.

Though our bodies enclose but a narrow space, let us rise high enough and our vision can embrace the world.

I want a friend as I want a book—always there at my bidding, attractive, entertaining, silent when I want. Alas, this is why I have more books than friends!

Neither constrict the body nor the spirit.

In taking a stroll, never worry where you walk as long as you have a world of thought to wander in.

Why do young women worry over their failure to make anything of themselves professionally, when this very failure testifies to their aptitude for what is most important to a woman—being a good wife and mother?

Many things are more enjoyable in retrospect than in reality.

I once spent a summer at Ruskin Manor, a residential hotel on Denmark Hill, in the south district of London. I was lonely and unhappy; and the other guests were a quiet, dignified, middle-class lot who were not of a kind to befriend a reticent young man. The only presence from whom I derived any pleasure was—as it became all too common in my life—a ghostly one, that of John Ruskin.

There he was, a delicate, pensive young man roaming about the rooms all day in a velvet-collared frock coat, gazing reverentially at his originals of Turner and Tintoretto that graced the Georgian mansion. An occasional visitor was Effie Gray, a gay Scottish girl for whom, when she was a child, he had written the fairy tale, "The King of the Golden River."

Poor Ruskin! Spoiled and dominated by his devoted but straight-laced parents. They disapproved of Effie. But he defied them for once and married her. It should have been a romantic story, but turned out an unhappy one, in which Ruskin's fame has suffered.

Mary Lutyens has told it well in "Young Mrs. Ruskin in Venice" and "Millais and the Ruskins." Their marriage was never consummated in the six years they lived together. Ruskin gave many reasons why he disdained relations—he did not want children, he wished he and his bride to be as virginal as the best exemplars of Christian living, and he was repelled by the sight of Effie on their honeymoon. He wrote privately years later: "Though her

APHORISMS AND REFLECTIONS

face was beautiful, her person was not formed to excite passion. On the contrary, there were certain circumstances in her person which completely checked it."

It is inconceivable that Ruskin, the great apostle of beauty in art, should have been unappreciative of beauty in women. Yet the evidence which has come to light a century later, in the writings of Miss Lutyens, Peter Quennell and Sir Williams James, is incontestable. His years of contemplating sculptures and paintings of women had, incredibly, unprepared him for the sight of a living nude.

He is an example of how too much purity in a person —too much conformance to an external code and not enough to the natural instincts of man—can destroy much that is beautiful and useful in that person's life—and, we may add, what may seem paradoxical,—so much of what is good. Ruskin was brought up in a stern, rigid atmosphere, typical of other Victorian homes. His great powers of observation and his ability to set down what he saw were developed to a fine degree. His writings are among the most beautiful examples of poetic prose in the language. But there was an aridity and stiffness in so much of his work that sprang from his failure to live life spontaneously and see it whole. Too late in his life he awoke to the truth that the greatest artists had been "a little wicked" and "boldly animal."

He was probably not impotent. As in many marriages like his, some of the blame must rest with a wife who perhaps did not exert her feminine charms to the utmost. There is, moreover, little evidence that Effie was made miserable by her husband's neglect as a lover. On the contrary, she is shown in her letters from Venice to have revelled in the freedom and independence conferred on her by a proud and trusting husband.

The conclusion is inescapable that Effie did not become discontented with Ruskin until she fell in love with the painter Millais. Yet she and Millais chose to blacken Ruskin's character to sustain the fiction that their friendship developed into love after Effie's annulment. Ruskin, gallantly, did nothing to explode this myth. And he continued to champion Millais after the painter's marriage to Effie.

It is curious to note that Effie and Millais afterwards lived a life of extreme Victorian respectability and conformity, in which Millais's art may well have suffered, while the solitary Ruskin continued to grow as an intellectual, perceptive and compassionate being, risking his reputation among the rich to champion the rights of the poor.

I cannot imagine the worldly Effie ever being happy with a social reformer who would go out and sweep the streets.

The trouble with many attempts at reconciliation is they are liable to succeed.

To be laughed at for absurdity by those who are themselves absurd, is to join in the laughter.

We never change from boyhood to manhood in our whims and irrationalities. We are only more adept at explaining ourselves.

For one person who is ready to fortify the confidence of another, there are a hundred ready to tear it down.

Observe how much better athletes perform when they have a mark to aim at, and how often the mark is excelled. Always let the seemingly impossible call forth your highest exertions.

One can be 100 per cent sincere in talking to one person, 50 per cent sincere in talking to two, and so on until we are wholly insincere in talking to many.

Nations spend billions to preserve their freedom. But what freedom? To be truly free is to be free from meanness, pettiness, superstition, jealousy, prejudice, and fear; and this is not within the power of nations, but individuals.

One can best attain goodluck—or should it be Godluck?—by acting in anticipation of it.

Draw out of the present moment the fullest joy it can offer, whether in the sight of a beautiful woman, a bird on the wing, a luminous moon peeping from behind gathering clouds.

Human beings are like bits of driftwood caught in a fast-flowing river, now tossed this way, now the other; now trapped in a whirling eddy, now dashed over a fall; sometimes sucked under the surface, only to reappear a little farther down; finally emerging into a placid stream and vanishing from sight.

What is so often discouraging about people is that, whenever they are confronted by a clear choice between right or wrong, they choose the wrong.

So many people of a restless, aggressive nature who have distinguished themselves in national emergencies, proving worthy of the highest honors, would deserve hanging in normal times.

Every day we are called upon to do professionally what we would shrink from personally—the journalist to write about something he finds distasteful, the lawyer to defend someone he deems worthless, the doctor to save a scoundrel he would rather let die.

What a superb artist is Nature! She paints in autumnal tints with as much richness and variety as if she had recourse to all the colors of the earth.

My dread is not so much the mischances that may befall me as my reaction to them. I have not yet evolved an attitude to life where I can be unmoved by what is disagreeable. Nor should I desire it if it should destroy my sensitivity to wrong or my anger at the wrongdoers.

Churchill has called courage the first of virtues. What idiocy! You will find courage in the schoolboy defying his teacher, the housebreaker defying the police, the murderer as he mounts the scaffold, the fool who leads a suicidal cavalry charge. When a nation has nothing but courage to praise, it is bankrupt morally.

Love imprisons the heart but liberates the spirit.

She stood at the graveside like a dutiful Christian, but in reality she was not; for she plucked branches from an evergreen tree to lay on the grave, robbing the living to adorn the dead.

One whose first aim in life is to be a wit seldom has the ability or character to be anything else.

This has been a Picassoic century—of abstraction, distortion, irreverence, grotesqueness and illusion—illusion that has turned, in life as in art, often into lunacy.

How often is the glimpse of a beautiful philosophy shattered by the glimpse of a beautiful woman?

There are people I have read about for whom I have formed such a deep affection that I have no desire to return to my reading of them, being content to dwell on them continually in my mind. Such it is with Cobden, Bright, Fox, the younger Pitt, Shelley, Milton, Sir Philip Sidney, Nelson, Clive,—but not Wellington, Montaigne, Thackeray, Sainte-Beuve, Keats, Ruskin, Jane Austen, Macaulay, Froude, Samuel Johnson, and Matthew Arnold, to whom I am as attached as to the others, but to whom I must be forever returning.

So it is with many friends—an initial impression so pleasing and overwhelming there is no incentive to pursue the friendship. And with places—one brief visit may suffice for a lifetime of reverie. In this, there is no fear of dulling the pleasure by returning. It is simply that I have acquired an immutable impression, which stands neither in need of refreshment nor in danger of diminution.

To write something so as to get it over with quickly, is much better than pondering it and taking one's time.

Ideas should be implanted quietly in minds we wish to change, instead of being imposed by force; for it is better for people—and nations—to believe they have come round to changes themselves than been reduced to accepting them from others.

No activity, no environment is agreeable unless it puts one in harmony with himself.

———

One of the most disturbing pastimes of life is watching people grow older, and feeling they are watching this in you.

———

Words unspoken are more eloquent than words that are.

———

Life is like a moderately long foot race—not for the impatient or the timid. The impatient start off with a burst of speed that shames their competitors and amazes the crowd; but they soon tire and are themselves overtaken. The timid can hardly get started at all for terror of the vista before them, quickly lose heart, and fall back among the stragglers. Only those finish triumphantly who adjust their pace to the distance, seeing the race neither as a sprint nor a marathon.

———

Jean Savant's "Napoleon In His Time" is the harshest indictment of Napoleon I have read. Napoleon the superpatriot, the lawgiver, the leader who sought to confer on Europe the blessings of the French Revolution, who plunged into war only because it would hasten the state of tranquillity he desired so much for his country, goes down forever before the testimony of people who knew him best. Now we see him, as surely as his own actions should have depicted him, as a brutal, cruel, ambitious, cynical, war-thirsty tyrant.

It is difficult to understand how, for a century and a half, this Corsican adventurer has commanded the admiration of the French, the very people whom he began life by hating. What a monstrous irony in those monuments they have raised to his memory! How much injury he has done to the genius of France!

All of us should be indebted to Savant for his diligence and courage in delivering what has been called a "coup de grace to a legend." The legend was begun by Napoleon himself at St. Helena, fearful of what posterity would say of his misdeeds. Savant denounces the exile's reminiscences as "a tissue of humbug," and like a skillful prosecutor has called forth a host of witnesses to belie them.

Napoleon said in his exile it was impossible, at the height of his power, to imitate the moderation, disinterestedness and wisdom of George Washington. The situation of France after the Revolution, he argued, was different to the situation of the American colonies after they became independent. The difference, however, was not so great that Napoleon, as First Consul, could not have bestowed peace on his country in the same way that Washington, as President, bestowed peace on his. But this would have meant Napoleon's renunciation of an emperor's crown and of his ambition to found a dynasty. These were more important to him than the peace and prosperity of France.

Fear is nothing more than a want of faith in God—a reluctance to entrust Him with things over which we have no control.

Is there anything more fascinating than the coming together of history and geography in the lives of such men as Marco Polo, Henry the Navigator, Columbus, Drake, and Captain Cook?

The family knelt at the grave with a side glance at

passersby to see if they remarked their piety. I could only murmur at their barbarism.

It is not the things which go right that amuse us most in looking back, but the things which go wrong.

Common sense is not always a blessing, for it puts the one who has it in a continual state of irritation at those who haven't.

There are two extremes of writing between which an aspiring stylist should steer—the artistic obsession of him who writes solely to vent his own impressions, thoughts and whims, without regard to the entertainment of others, and the eagerness of the journalist to communicate everything of interest to others, without regard to the sensibilities of himself.

The thoughts of contemporary philosophers might be likened to mountain water which they have imbibed in all its freshness, only to urinate indiscriminately on everything, and call it good.

Alone, indifferent to the few people who listened to him and the many more who tried not to, the maniac poured out a torrent of vituperation for twenty-five minutes on a crowded ferryboat, shouting, raving and weeping, never once making sense and never once at a loss for a word. How easily, with only a trifle less madness, could such a one pass as an accomplished orator—another Hitler or Mussolini—and lead and deceive millions.

Anyone can be courteous, thoughtful and decent to others when the going is good. But when it is not?

It is pleasant to be a frontrow spectator at the drama of life, provided none of the action spills over from the stage.

Some people don't mind expressing wicked things so long as they don't have to perform them; others don't mind performing them if they can refrain from expressing them.

Beauty, simplicity and naturalness—strive for these in your life and everything else will follow.

I have visited the field of Waterloo twice. Nowhere has there been a stage of human action where men have been pitted together in a more dramatic encounter. Napoleon—ruthless, overbearing, vainglorious and theatrical, eager to "measure myself with Wellington." Wellington—serene, confident, clearsighted, undismayed by Napoleon's fast descent on him. Blucher—rough and coarse but one of those rare men who give their word and keep it.

The night before the battle—not the night of the Brussels ball, which was three days before, but a dreadful night of torrential rain and dark forebodings—is illustrative of the three men. Blucher at Wavre, sending midnight word to Wellington he would be there the next morning. Wellington at his inn in Waterloo, calmly writing letters and dispatches up to 1 a.m. before going to bed. Napoleon at his Le Caillou farmhouse six miles away, rising at 1 a.m. because he was too excited to

sleep and dashing about in the rain to assure himself the
enemy were there to be crushed the next morning.

Two of Wellington's officers wait on him nervously to
inquire what his plans are for the battle in the event he
is killed. The Iron Duke receives them kindly. How can
he tell what his plans are, he answers, when nobody
knows what Napoleon will do the next morning? So they
go away, satisfied the battle will be like so many of Wellington's brilliant improvisations.

On my second visit, I walked from the inn of Le Belle
Alliance, near which Napoleon surveyed the battle in the
last critical hours, to the crossroads at the top of the
ridge, where Wellington sat much of the time on horse-
back under an elm tree, watching wave after wave of
French troops hurling themselves on his dwindling forces,
and waiting for the Prussians under Blucher to come.
They came when it was getting dark, and the carnage by
then must have been awful—fields of dying men and
horses, the groans and screams of the wounded, the smell
of dead and gunpowder hanging over it all.

Why am I, a detester of war, so drawn to this scene?
Undoubtedly from an admiration of Wellington, a man
who hated it too. The British nation showered him with
honors and raised many monuments to his memory. But
they never took him to their hearts. Philip Guedalla
thinks it was because he was too successful. The British
like their heroes, he wrote, to be like Nelson, who at
least atoned for success by falling in the hour of victory.

In 1914, when the Francophiles dominated so much of
Britain's political and military thinking, it was not to the
strategy of the victorious Wellington that they turned—
the strategy of a highly mobile army linked to seapower
—but to the mass frontal attacks of Napoleon's decline.
How stupid can a nation's leaders be?

But Wellington has much to teach us in everyday living. He has said somewhere that his victories were due

to the application of common sense to the circumstances of the moment. Such a prescription must imply the fullest reliance on the resources within us, always greater than we imagine, and a modicum of commitment to allow the greatest freedom of action.

Someone once asked Wellington how he succeeded in defeating one after another of the great marshals whom Napoleon sent against him in Spain. "I will tell you," said the Duke. "They planned their campaigns just as you might make a splendid set of harness. It looks very well and answers very well until it gets broken, and then you are done for. Now I made my campaigns of rope. If anything went wrong, I tied a knot and went on."

Wellington had the reputation of being a cold, irreligious man. He was not. Much of his serenity came from a deep sense of religion. One of the paintings he captured from the baggage of Joseph Bonaparte on the French retreat from Madrid was Correggio's "Agony in the Garden." He never failed to draw calm and inspiration from it in moments of stress. The Bourbons of Spain allowed him to keep it with other intercepted masterpieces, and it is still to be seen in Wellington's old London home, Apsley House.

One's mind should be like a splendid palace, spacious, elegant and cheerful, filled with a variety of rooms into which one can retire according to his mood, uncluttered with old and ugly furnishings, adorned with everything that is beautiful.

Hate destroys, love creates.

A story is told of the great newspaper publisher Joseph Pulitzer, disgusted by the dull perfection into which the

New York World had fallen. One day he ordered his business manager to hire some newspaper man who had the reputation of being habitually drunk and let him have carte blanche to stir things up in the office. Such a man was hired and the paper took on new life. Pulitzer had hit on a truth with universal application—that people and institutions can perish from an excess of respectability. Look at the United Nations today, serene, stately, dignified—and dying. Look at great shops, businesses and universities—sound, well-organized, stable and orderly, but often more intent at earning respect than engaging in the rough-and-tumble of service. How many churches suffer from the same tomb-like gentility—a minister moving pleasantly among his congregation, a congregation well-dressed and well-mannered; but no involvement, no controversy, no explosiveness.

One of the most damaging charges against a man is that he is immature. Thank God for that, I say, if he has retained the enthusiasm, freshness, eagerness and wonder of childhood.

Some people are much better at stating a problem than overcoming it.

It is wrong to judge something in isolation, without weighing what has preceded.

Those who are given to seeing everything sexually and expressing it vulgarly possess pitifully narrow minds, unreceptive to all that is fine and beautiful in the world.

Behind the facade of civilized behavior, one is conscious of the hate, cruelty and evil ready to burst forth.

There are reticences that wound more deeply than the cruelest utterances.

Ours is not an affluent society so much as an acquisitive one.

Why does a girl seated sedately in a train, dressed quietly, her long dark hair framing a pretty but expressionless face, exude more excitement and charm than a flashy creature who bounces about seductively?

I have had experience in avoiding experiences.

One of our continual mistakes is taking light things seriously and serious things lightly.

To be completely affable, one must be completely insincere.

A distressing manifestation of our time is the frequency with which nations and individuals, knowingly and almost eagerly, act against their own best interests.

So much of what is committed in the name of freedom is but insistence on the right to make money.

How often is physical courage but an exhibition of stupidity!

There are times when, for the sake of a country's wellbeing, a strong government must act against the wishes of its people. But the effect of its contrariness must be evident to all very quickly. Otherwise, national confidence will collapse. This, then, would be an autocratic democracy, a seeming contradiction of terms, but the only form of effective government.

A fault that can be tolerated in another a continent away cannot be endured when near.

Strive to be attuned to all Nature.

There is more Christianity in the tiny Borromini church of the Trinitarian Order in Rome, with its history of help to prisoners of the Moslems, than in all the vast Cathedral of St. Peter's.

How quickly the persecuted become the persecutors!

Beware of losing the essence of an object of interest by too close attention to detail.

To see life dramatically, as in a theatre, we must pause occasionally and see it concentrated—on a street, at a bar, in a restaurant,—extracting from the scene, no matter how fleeting, as much interest as we can, always incomplete, for that is life.

An intense moment of joy can redeem a month of unhappiness.

One of the secrets of a happy life is to be content with little.

The instinctive reaction of most people confronted by an idea is to think of a host of reasons to reject it.

We lose so much by striving for so much.

Too many races and nationalities—English, Scotch, Americans, Jews, negroes,—are prejudiced not so much *against* others as *for* themselves, glorying in habits and traits that often, in reality, are narrow and mean, and so cutting themselves off from what is noblest in the world.

Bad examples often serve us better than the good.

The curse of our time is the increasing number of people who have the ability to speak but not to think.

Drugs and alcohol are only synthetic ways of attaining the exhilaration, cheerfulness, confidence and sense of wellbeing that come from closeness to God.

What is being close to God? It is being close to everything that is alive, everything that is beautiful, everything that incites us to kindness and generosity.

Women should learn the difference between practicing seduction and being seductive.

Look on everyday things with the excitement of one coming from a distant place.

A man should marry as quietly as he is born.

At the end of the day, I go to my favorite authors as many go to a cocktail party—listening solemnly to one person, laughing with another, moving on eagerly to a third, ending by being pleasantly drunk from it all.

Think of religion as a well by which we dip deeply into the resources within us.

The more I know some people, the dearer to me are my cats.

Only awaken curiosity and you awaken energy, courage, enterprise and zeal.

This is a generation that has invented a host of ways to circumvent common sense.

Religion is not a Sunday thing but is as much a part of our lives as food and drink—something we can do without, but at our peril.

We should take care never to gain perfect happiness, for then we have nothing to look forward to.

I yield to no one in my admiration of Henry James. He is the supreme literary craftsman, spinning his tales out of vague hints and suggestions with an art illuminating to every writer. But "The Portrait of a Lady," by some considered his masterpiece—here is where I differ from other Jamesians. I found the novel shoddy, tedious and longwinded. I fear myriads of young people have been diverted from James by such an introduction to his works.

As in so many stories of Henry James, he has sacrificed almost all the elements of good fiction to his theme. And even his theme is bad. The only chance of the reader's interest being roused and sustained is in the central character, Isabel Archer; and James had made of her a dull, vapid young woman, without a particle of charm.

Catherine Sloper is reminiscent of her in "Washington Square." But this was a much superior novel, even though James thought so little of it that he excluded it from his deluxe New York Edition. It was superior because it was believable. Catherine engaged our sympathy. Held down by a tyrannical father, she desperately needed a happy marriage; and the only man she loved was a vile fortune-hunter.

Isabel Archer, equally well off, is pursued by wealthy suitors such as an English lord, an American industrialist and an international banker's son. But what in heaven's name did any of them see in her? Her personality is colorless; her intelligence is weak; her manners are atrocious; her physical appeal is nowhere apparent. Catherine's fortune-hunter, Morris Townsend, would have overlooked these deficiencies. The reader is not so fortunate.

James never learned to compress. Development of his theme, he wrote once, was his temptation and his joy. In this art, when performed within proper bounds, he is unrivalled. But his theme in "The Portrait of a Lady" was a thin one—it was like a bucket of paint that would have done admirably for a garden pavilion but was inadequate for a manor house.

He could have reduced the novel by half—to the length, say, of "Washington Square"—with a possible gain in narrative flow, certainly in a shrinkage of the reader's boredom.

It is all very well to point to the stiffness of manners

and the adherence to convention in the Victorian time as an apology for this novel. But the Victorians were alive. They were capable of immense good, of immense strivings. They were more than sufficient to have floated "a frail vessel" like Isabel Archer in vast seas of excitement. But it would have required more of life than James was willing to give her.

One can be a miser with books as much as a miser with money, gloating over what he has accumulated, greedy for more, mindless of his responsibilities to others, and above all forgetful that books, like riches, are merely a means to something nobler.

I have admired more women than I have loved. But what woman wants only to be admired?

Politicians need only the qualities of good actors to get by in this world—a prepossessing appearance, readiness to adapt to any role, the ability to deliver other men's lines, a flair for showmanship.

A garrulous person who has something to say is far worse than one who has nothing—the latter you don't have to listen to.

"The best is yet to be," proclaimed Browning. The best is here and now.

Suppressing an enthusiasm is like slamming the phone down on God.

It is always pleasing to be given credit for good intentions without the bother of carrying them out.

We complain at a friend "letting us down" by failing to live up to what we expected of him. We should complain, rather, at our own failure to see him rightly.

Those moments are best that inspire us with a prayer of thankfulness.

How wretchedly has our time dealt with the meaning of stranger!—formerly one to be helped and sheltered, now one to be mistrusted and kept out.

Something praiseworthy that we do will more quickly excite jealousy than praise.

Why is it that some women—lazy, dull, unexciting—can inspire men with the most beautiful dreams? Ah, why puzzle? It is the dreams that matter.

Cars only serve to take people farther from themselves.

Schools breed two types of people equally handicapped for life—the brilliant students who get a sense of superiority that invests them with too much confidence, and the slow learners who get a sense of inferiority that invests them with too little.

New-glimpsed ideas are like those amphibious, naked,

writhing shapes plucked howling from the sea by mythological heroes, puzzled whether they had a monster or a mermaid by the tail.

If in doubt about something, wait until the moment of commission, then if the doubts persist—if an overwhelming sense of misgiving arises—give it up.

One of the ironies of my life as a bachelor is that I am pursued by women I wish to forget and forgotten by women I wish to pursue.

Have not many men become successful in politics not because of any capacity for public life but because of incapacity for simple living?

Men crave romance, women marriage.

The surest way to guard against frustration, disappointment, rudeness and bitterness is to isolate oneself from people. But one may as well hang himself.

It is with some women as it is with certain books— with everything to make them desirable they fail to excite desire.

I have possessed from earliest remembrance what I call a Noah's Ark mind—a mind which conjures up delicious fancies of farseeing, diligent people gathered into one secure, pleasant spot, such as a remote island, a Boccaccio-like villa or a fortress-castle, with misery and evil everywhere outside, happiness within. How often have these fancies shaped my ideas!

How idiotic were the intruders who ransacked my library for hidden wealth, which glittered before them all the while from three score shelves!

I have never feared discovery in actions that others may think reprehensible, only lack of opportunity to explain them.

Robert Louis Stevenson has likened quiet people to clocks that go on ticking in thunderstorms. Too many quiet people nowadays are like electric clocks that stop in one.

"Men of Concord" gives a displeasing picture of Thoreau. One can scarcely recognize the author of "Walden," the man who fronted only the essential facts of life and enjoined everyone to stand forth free and uncommitted. Here he appears to flee from the company of gentlemen to mingle with a trivial breed. The rebuke once administered to him, of being a "cold, intellectual skeptic," who preferred to commit his thoughts to his diary rather than share them generously with a friend, seems herein to have been richly deserved. He was not a joyful, exuberant philosopher like Horace. If a bore had accosted him in the Concord woods, as one did Horace in the Roman Forum, Thoreau would doubtless have embraced him as a long-lost friend and taken him home.

The book is made up entirely of extracts from Thoreau's own notebooks. The emphasis of the editor, F. H. Allen, is on what Thoreau saw of his neighbors. We cannot help thinking they were, by and large, a mean-spirited lot, little deserving of his time or observation. How different are these extracts from those edited by Odell Shepard in "The Heart of Thoreau's Journals."

What we saw there was a reporter of the interior life. That was far more important to Thoreau, and more interesting to us, than the world of his neighbors. He was, in his own phrase, "too cold for human friendship." He thrived on solitude. He delighted in poverty with the ardor of a saint. We are charmed and elevated by his writings. But we should have run away from Thoreau himself.

Craziness was once an affliction to be avoided. Now it is a blessing to be cultivated.

Serenity and marriage are as unmixable as oil and fire.

When a smell persists, it is best to examine our own shoes.

Ignorance detracts from the appeal of a man, adds to it in a woman.

The more encounters I have with people the more I am diminished in myself, as a cake of soap dissolves from repeated immersions, so that finally I lose all identity and become a conglomerate of many. How does one survive? Simply by communing with oneself as frequently as with others.

Children are never embarrassed when they are seen naked. Why, then, should grownups be?

There are two reasons for prayer—when we can do something and when we can't. When we can, prayer strengthens us. When we can't, it sustains us.

I like what was said of a young woman—"She has the ability to wonder at things."

The inward life and the outward—how different! Yet each should influence the other to the degree that neither disturbs the harmony, quietness and happiness of the complete person.

So often we strive for blessings we lack and overlook those we have.

Beware of the busy man. Often he is so engrossed in urgent matters that he has no time for what is really important—keeping his mind and heart open to love and beauty and understanding.

We are always most successful when we are completely thrown back on ourselves. Britain's finest hour in the last war was not when she was supported by friends but when she was beset by enemies. Crusoe would have gone to pieces if he had been dependent on a flock of fellow castaways, jealous, distrustful and quarrelsome.

Too many women are provoking without being provocative.

To succeed in the art of making money, one must combine the talents of a confidence man, a thief, a swindler and a cut-throat, while adhering to the aspect of a gentleman.

People always relish an element of danger in something they undertake, like seeing what looks like a savage beast at a distance, which turns out to be—if they care to look closely—an overgrown cat.

To remain young, one must be continually in love.

The chief value of a college education should be a love of books. But how often do young people come away with a lifetime horror of them? Can we wonder at it when educators force the best books on their students with an injunction to study and dissect them? Dissect them! To dissect "Pilgrim's Progress," the poems of Keats, "The Alhambra," "Vanity Fair"! It is like grabbing a young woman from the street, chloroforming her, dumping her on an operating table, and handing scalpels to students to see what makes her beautiful. There is only one way to make young people love good books and that is by rousing their curiosity for them. Then leave the young ones alone.

A woman is only an animated being when most like a predatory animal. When her pursuit is over—when she captures her man or whatever she is after—then the animation fades, and she is apt to settle back into passivity and dullness.

Forgetting is as vital to our wellbeing as learning— more so, in fact, as we get older, when so much of what we have assimilated needs to be tossed out, as one would empty a garbage pail.

Is there such a thing as time? The subconscious, the very core of our being, does not acknowledge it. Witness our dreams, in which those who are dead mingle naturally with those still alive.

We often say "Use your head" when, more properly, it should be "Use your heart."

Who has left his impress more deeply on British 20th Century history than any other man? Winston Churchill? Lloyd George? No, Henry Wilson by a long shot. If only a few Americans have heard of him, neither have the majority of his countrymen.

Sir Henry Wilson was a Protestant Irishman who entered the British army as a youth, served in India, and sustained a scar across the forehead—and lasting head-aches—when a Burmese hit him on the head with an ax. He fought in the Boer War; and in 1910, when he was 46 and considered one of the most brilliant men in the army, he became Director of Military Operations.

He was a scoffer par excellence. His boss at the War Office was "poor old Nick," the Secretary of War "a funny old thing," the Foreign Secretary a "funk," and a military paper submitted by Home Secretary Winston Churchill "ridiculous and fantastic." This giant in khaki sneered at everyone and everything with the exception of the French, whom he loved, and one Frenchman in particular, General Foch, whom he adored.

Foch, one of France's leading military theorists as head of the war college, and Wilson, who visited him frequently, agreed that preparations should start immediately for a war of "revanche" against Germany and that the British must mobilize the same day as the French, whether any threat was posed to the neutrality of Belgium, Britain's prime object of Continental concern. The two drew up elaborate plans for six British divisions to move swiftly into line on the left flank of the French.

Once, while cycling through the French countryside on a vacation, Wilson tore off a bit of the map showing the proposed areas of British concentration, and laid it reverently at the foot of a statue representing France, overlooking the 1870 Metz battlefield. There is no record of a spy picking it up. But most of the chancelleries of Europe knew Wilson and the French were plotting war long before it was known to the British cabinet or Parliament.

Foch came to London at Wilson's invitation, and the two men had a great time damning the politicians, whom Wilson called the Frocks, and his military superiors, whom he called the Brasshats. Wilson showed Foch a model of the Battle of Waterloo, and Foch sneered at that. His hero was Napoleon, who lost the battle, not Wellington, who won it. In fact, they pooh-poohed all the great captains from Alexander to Frederick. They pooh-poohed the influence of sea power. They pooh-poohed the lessons of the American Civil War. They pooh-poohed planes and other modern weaponry. All that mattered was to assemble the biggest army possible, make contact with the main force of the enemy as quickly as you could, and keep hammering away until it surrendered or disintegrated.

Once in France, when Wilson quoted a military expert as saying the British navy would be worth half a million bayonets to the French army when war came, Foch replied that it wouldn't be worth one. Wilson agreed.

It is hard to explain the influence of this rude, ignorant, undistinguished British general on his contemporaries. But the evidence is overwhelming. Wilson converted everyone. His achievement was all the more remarkable in the prewar years when Germany, feeling the economic pressure of a naval race with Britain, was beginning to lose her arrogance and make friendly overtures to the Asquith Government.

On a hot August day in 1911 Wilson presided over a secret meeting of the Committee of Imperial Defense, at which some members of the cabinet heard for the first time how far staff conversations with the French had gone. With a large map and a pointer, Sir Henry talked through lunchtime. The First Sea Lord, Sir Arthur (Tug) Wilson, followed in the afternoon. He made it plain, in blunt sailor language, that, in the event of war, his ships would not be a tail-kite to Henry Wilson's six divisions and that the British navy would adhere to its traditional policy of landing fast-moving forces where the enemy least expected them. Sir Henry sneered at that. So did the Prime Minister, the Foreign Secretary, the War Secretary and Home Secretary Churchill.

The aftermath was a golf match, which should rank next to Drake's pre-Armada game of bowls as the most famous game in British history. On the links overlooking the Firth of Forth, the Prime Minister offered the post of First Lord of the Admiralty to Churchill on the understanding that he dump that antiquated sea dog Tug Wilson and bring naval plans into line with those of brilliant Henry Wilson. Churchill, a former cavalryman, accepted with boyish exuberance.

Of Henry Wilson's triumph, the British military historian Liddell Hart has written: "Its most far-reaching effect was not in France but in England. There is no exaggeration in saying that it diverted the course of English history—because it revolutionized the traditional war policy of the island kingdom."

In the crisis of July and August, 1914, when Asquith's Liberal Government looked as if it might be split wide open over the French commitment, Wilson intrigued to bring the Conservatives into power. But it was not necessary. The Germans got Asquith "off the hook" by striking at France first through Belgium.

When Sir Henry went to say goodbye to Churchill before leaving for France, Churchill burst into tears. But Wilson lived through the holocaust. He saw the coming of Kitchener's million, whom he called "the laughing stock of Europe," and of the Americans, whom he derided with a remark to one of their officers: "Now are you too proud to fight?"

He sneered at the "nauseating nonsense about peace" at the end of four years of slaughter, resigned from the War Office in 1922 rather than join in talks with the Americans for a mutual reduction of armaments, and died on his London doorstep a few months later at the hands of Irish assassins.

The best way to deal with irritations is to ignore them. The letter that disturbs you. What if you had never received it? The story in the newspaper that angers you. What if you had never read it? The irritating incident related by a friend. What if he had omitted to tell you? Cultivate a state of mind that rises so far above petty upsets that they disappear altogether, like watching a city full of noise and agitation from the tranquillity of a plane or mountaintop.

Columbus, in his discovery of the New World, suffered more from the contrarieties of man than he ever did from those of Nature.

One can only dedicate himself to fulfilling the wants of others after he has fulfilled his own. Alas, it has taken me most of my life to do that!

Beautiful women are like fire—fascinating to watch, wonderful to be near, always glowing if well attended to, dangerous when left alone.

Are not our delusions more substantial to us, almost more precious, than realities?

Is not most of life making the best of bad situations?

The mind always fixes upon some worry, usually trivial, which once removed another replaces. Recognize this and the worries cease.

How wrong it is to charge anyone with a specific offense when his whole character cries out against it.

The trouble with leaders who profess a love for people is that they are ready to sacrifice them to their love.

Tension is simply a state of future tense—thinking too much of what lies ahead and not sufficiently of what lies at hand.

I find very often I have formed an unfavorable impression of someone before meeting him that I am inclined to dismiss when I do. But why should that be? Is not an impression resulting from a cool contemplation of facts more trustworthy than one gained face to face, in which charm, or even ill manners, may beguile the judgment?

Large temptations we can resist; the small undo us.

People fight for small distinctions when they are unable to obtain the great.

The Irish would be better for English sobriety, the English for Irish exuberance.

How often are we repelled by a great man simply because we have known him or read about him in his sedate old age, forgetting that his struggles and achievements may have occurred in a fresh, vigorous, attractive youth, as with Darwin, Longfellow, Wordsworth, Browning, and Robert Frost.

Always remember you are a child of God, and whenever thoughts arise in you of love and beauty, they are whispers of your divinity.

It is foolish to deliberate too long over a problem. Too much thinking, too much mulling over facts, tend to swamp our judgment and common sense.

One's character should be formed like a well-built, well-handled ship—strong against storm and stress, obedient to every change of course, able to go where it pleases, containing within itself all that makes for safety, sustenance and pleasure.

Make use of the resources you have—they are always considerable.

A longwinded book, a wearying conversation, a tedious play pose a threat to my personal liberty more terrifying than political despotism.

To protect people from the consequences of their own follies is to commit the worst of all follies.

I left a man in need of a friendly chat to address a prayer to God. It ended in neither hearing me.

Americans go to the polls every four years to elect a President and end up with a Commander-in-Chief.

A perpetual state of optimism is the sure mark of a fool.

One of the most unrecognized motives of human conduct is the element of excitement. It takes on many disguises. It is seen in sports, gambling, mountain-climbing, exploring, crime, and war. It is a craving in people for something to rouse their lives from dull monotony. The wars of Charles V of Spain and Francis I of France are instructive of how this element of excitement could set a whole continent afire. There was no stake important enough to justify either country's expenditure of treasure and blood. The flimsiest pretexts were employed for the most warlike deeds. The two kings rode out to war as they rode out to hunt. "Francis and I," remarked Charles once, "have a great deal in common—we both want Milan." This same element of excitement operates in international affairs today. But unscrupulous rulers are more cunning in rationalizing it, and unlike Charles and Francis have always an inexhaustible supply of money to draw on from deluded subjects.

I would much sooner write to old friends than see them. The outward changes that have occurred in them since last I saw them may in no manner correspond to the inner person I have known and loved. Yet my attention would be diverted to these changes, as theirs to mine.

Eavesdrop on conversations in restaurants and trains and note how seldom they touch on public events. When they do, it is like the weather—there is nothing better to talk about.

Do you crave independence? Never borrow. Never seek favors.

I have passed the age where I wish to experiment or explore. My life has become an ecstatic re-tasting of former pleasures—old friendships, old authors, old works of art and music, old wines, old places.

A surfeit of facts can smother the imagination as easily as an excess of gas can stall a car.

Worries are like snarling dogs—stand and face them and they turn and run.

An optimist and a pessimist have this in common— they are doomed to perpetual disappointment.

Most politicians are no better than radio or television broadcasters, who one moment are extolling a new model car and the next peddling a deodorant.

How much superior we think ourselves to the dog who scavenges all day for food and finally trots off with a dirty bone. But are not most of us, less obviously but with the same lack of refinement, engaged in the same pursuit?

Why do Americans read Francis Parkman so little?

He is the greatest of their historians. He has the same blending of scenery with history that we find in Walter Scott. He was a lover of the American forest. The wilderness haunted him. He longed to write about it and to roam through it and to make people thrill to it as he did. This he eminently achieves. The loneliness, the terror and the mystery of the forest are present in all his histories, giving them a peculiar merit all their own. Men are not battling and intriguing against one another, as in the history of courts, but are battling and intriguing against Nature herself. And when you have a hero like La Salle, who fights against man, disease and Nature for a lofty ideal, never admitting defeat, carrying on against heartbreaking disasters and discouragements with courage and fortitude, you have a history that rises both to scenic and dramatic heights.

What makes fools so dangerous is that, in everything they say, there is always a modicum of truth.

The chief difficulty in achieving a happy, successful life is in striking a balance between divine selfhood—thinking sufficiently of oneself—and unselfish dedication—thinking sufficiently of others.